OUR JOURNEY AFTER LIFE

RAJESH
VIJAYAKUMAR

INDIA • SINGAPORE • MALAYSIA

ISBN 979-8-89186-599-0

Contents

Preamble

I would like to thank GOD for showering blessings to write this book.

Once I decided to write a book having various thoughts on the topics and finally chosen this as "***Our journey after life***" I personally realised and recognized that for every human being a journey after life is paramount importance, however no one bother about that because the life what we live now is the life which can be seen but the life after this life is really unknown a subject of profound fascination and contemplation.

Therefore, no one is accepting the life after our actual life. To understand this, we need to realize that we are just a soul not the body which we possess. Irrespective of beliefs and religion, the concept of soul is accepted and various literature also taught us on this.

In this journey my elder son Master Koushik had helped me a lot by kept asking am I completed the book as mentioned earlier. He has been a motivation for me to write this book.

I would like to grateful to my wife Mrs. Anuratha without her support I would have not written this book.

Finally, I would like to thank the readers who reads this book.

This book gives understanding of life to the soul even after our current life (life of body), and we can definitely choose our destination after our real life.

* * * * * *

CHAPTER – 1

Introduction to the Life

In material world, there are two sets of people one who shows more eager to know about the future and another set of people where always things about the past. But in reality no one is happy about the present life.

1.1 The present life is a beautiful if you realize

Life, in all its complexity and diversity, is a remarkable phenomenon that has fascinated humanity since time immemorial. It is the essence of our existence, the force that propels us forward, and the canvas upon which we paint the stories of our existence. This chapter serves as an exploration, an introduction to the intricate tapestry of life, delving into its many dimensions, from the biological to the philosophical, and examining the profound questions it raises about our existence.

Life is a magnificent tapestry woven with a myriad of experiences, emotions, and moments that shape our existence. It's easy to get caught up in the hustle and bustle of everyday life, often overlooking the beauty that surrounds us. Amidst the challenges and trials, life reveals its true splendour when we pause to realize and appreciate the blessings that come our way.

1.2 The power of perspectives

Perspective is a powerful lens through which we view the world. Life's challenges can be overwhelming, but when we shift our perspective, difficulties transform into opportunities for growth and learning. Embracing a positive mindset doesn't mean ignoring the struggles; it means acknowledging them and choosing to focus on the lessons they offer.

1.3 Gratitude: A Gateway to Happiness

Gratitude is a universal language that can be spoken by anyone, anywhere, regardless of their circumstances. When we cultivate gratitude, we open the door to happiness and contentment. It's about appreciating the little things—a warm cup of tea on a cold morning, a genuine smile from a stranger, or the soothing sound of rain tapping on your window. Practicing gratitude allows us to find beauty in simplicity and joy in the ordinary.

1.4 Embracing Imperfections

Life is imperfect, and so are we. Our flaws and mistakes are an integral part of who we are. Embracing our imperfections with self-compassion and understanding enables us to live authentically. It's in our vulnerabilities that we find strength, and in our mistakes that we discover wisdom. Realizing that imperfection is a shared human experience connects us to others, fostering empathy and compassion in our relationships.

1.5 Cherishing Relationships

Some of life's most beautiful moments are shared with the people we love. Building meaningful connections and nurturing relationships enrich our lives in ways that material possessions never can. Whether it's family, friends, or romantic partners, the love and support we give and receive create a profound sense of fulfillment. Realizing the beauty in these relationships reminds us of the importance of love, kindness, and companionship in our journey.

1.6 The Beauty of Nature and Simplicity

Nature has an inherent beauty that captivates the soul. The gentle rustle of leaves, the vibrant colours of a sunset, or the rhythmic crashing of waves against the shore—all these elements remind us of the awe-inspiring wonders of the natural world. Taking a moment to connect with nature, even in the midst of urban life, can bring a profound sense of peace and appreciation for the beauty that exists outside of human creation.

1.7 Finding Purpose and Meaning

Life gains profound meaning when we discover our purpose and contribute positively to the world. Whether it's through a fulfilling career, creative expression, volunteering, or acts of kindness, realizing that our actions can make a difference adds depth and significance to our existence. By aligning our passions with our actions, we create a life that is not only beautiful for ourselves but also for those around us.

Life is undeniably beautiful if we take the time to realize it. Cultivating gratitude, embracing imperfections, cherishing relationships, connecting with nature, and finding purpose are essential elements that enhance the beauty of our existence. When we approach life with a positive mindset and an open heart, even the simplest moments become precious treasures, reminding us of the extraordinary beauty that resides within the ordinary. So, let us cherish every moment, learn from every experience, and embrace the beauty of life in all its forms.

1.8 The Biological Essence of Life

At its most fundamental level, life is a biological phenomenon. It is characterized by a set of processes and attributes that distinguish living organisms from inanimate matter. The hallmark of life is the capacity for growth, reproduction, and adaptation. Living organisms possess a genetic code, the blueprint of their existence, which is passed down from one generation to the next.

Life on Earth is incredibly diverse, with millions of species inhabiting a wide range of environments, from the deepest oceans to the highest mountains, and from scorching deserts to frozen polar regions. The mechanisms of life are deeply rooted in the molecular and cellular processes that govern everything from the simplest single-celled organisms to the most complex multicellular beings.

Life, in all its diverse forms and complexities, is one of the most intriguing phenomena in the universe. From the tiniest microorganisms to the grandeur of complex organisms, the biological essence of life has fascinated scientists, philosophers, and thinkers throughout the ages. At its core, life is a masterpiece of intricate biochemical processes, governed by the fundamental principles of biology. Let's embark on a journey to unravel the mysteries of this biological essence of life.

1.9 The Blueprint of Life: DNA and Genetic Information

At the heart of every living organism lies a remarkable molecule called **Deoxyribonucleic Acid**, or **DNA**. DNA serves as the biological blueprint, containing the instructions necessary for the growth, development, functioning, and reproduction of all known living organisms. The sequence of nucleotides in DNA strands forms genes, which encode specific proteins, the building blocks of life. This elegant system of information storage and retrieval is the foundation upon which life's diversity is built.

1.10 Cellular Complexity: The Basic Unit of Life

The cell is the basic structural and functional unit of life. Every organism, whether a single-celled bacterium or a complex multicellular organism like a human, is composed of cells. Within these microscopic entities, an orchestra of biochemical reactions takes place, allowing life to sustain itself. Cells carry out processes such as metabolism, growth, response to stimuli, and reproduction. The intricate machinery within cells, including organelles like mitochondria and the endoplasmic reticulum, facilitates these vital functions.

1.11 Energy Currency: Adenosine Triphosphate (ATP)

Life requires energy, and the primary energy currency in biological systems is Adenosine Triphosphate, or ATP. Through cellular respiration, organisms extract energy from nutrients and convert it into ATP. This energy is then utilized to power various biological processes, enabling everything from muscle contraction to nerve signalling. The ability to generate and utilize energy is a defining characteristic of living systems.

1.12 Evolution: The Engine of Biodiversity

The biological essence of life is intrinsically linked to the process of evolution. Over billions of years, life on Earth has undergone remarkable transformations, leading to the incredible biodiversity we observe today. The theory of evolution, proposed by Charles Darwin, explains how species evolve over time through the process of natural selection. This fundamental principle of biology underscores the interconnectedness of all living organisms and highlights the adaptability and resilience of life.

1.13 Homeostasis: Maintaining Balance in Living Systems

Living organisms have a remarkable ability to maintain internal stability despite changes in their external environment—a phenomenon known as homeostasis. This delicate balance is crucial for the survival and functioning of biological systems. From temperature regulation in mammals to the pH balance in our bloodstream, homeostasis ensures that living organisms can thrive in diverse and often challenging environments.

1.14 The Interconnected Web of Life

Beyond individual organisms, life exists within intricate ecosystems where various species interact with one another and their environment. The balance of these ecosystems is delicate, with each organism playing a unique role. From pollinators ensuring the reproduction of plants to predators controlling population sizes, every living entity is interconnected, emphasizing the interdependence of life on Earth.

In essence, life is a symphony of biochemical processes, cellular intricacies, energy transformations, evolutionary adaptations, and ecological interactions. Understanding the biological essence of life not only deepens our appreciation for the natural world but also inspires further exploration and discovery. As scientists continue to unravel the mysteries of life, we gain valuable insights into our origins, our place in the natural world, and our responsibility to preserve the extraordinary diversity of life on Earth.

1.15 The Evolutionary Dance

Life on Earth is a grand dance, a choreography of constant change and adaptation that has been unfolding for billions of years. This intricate ballet, known as evolution, is the fundamental mechanism through which all living organisms have emerged and diversified. The evolutionary dance is a testament to the resilience, creativity, and perpetual motion of life, shaping the natural world in ways both breathtaking and awe-inspiring.

The story of life on Earth is also a narrative of evolution. Over billions of years, life has undergone a continuous process of change and adaptation. Charles Darwin's theory of evolution by natural selection provided a groundbreaking framework for understanding how life diversifies and evolves.

Life's diversity is a testament to the power of evolution, as species adapt to their environments, develop new traits, and sometimes face extinction. The process of evolution is a dynamic and ongoing dance of genetic variation and selection, a testament to the incredible resilience of life.

1.16 The Ancient Steps of Evolution

The origins of the evolutionary dance can be traced back to the primordial soup of early Earth, where simple organic molecules began to assemble and form the first living entities. Over eons, these microscopic life forms, from bacteria to algae, waltzed through the ancient oceans, paving the way for more complex life to emerge. Through the process of natural selection, advantageous traits were favored, leading to an ever-expanding array of species, each uniquely adapted to its environment.

1.17 Adaptation: Nature's Choreography

Central to the evolutionary dance is adaptation, the elegant process by which organisms tailor their traits to suit the demands of their environment. Whether it's the long neck of a giraffe reaching for high branches or the camouflage of a chameleon blending seamlessly with its surroundings, adaptation allows species to thrive amidst challenges.

The dance of evolution is shaped by the intricate interplay between genetic variation, environmental pressures, and the survival of the fittest, sculpting life in remarkable and unexpected ways

1.18 Biodiversity: Nature's Masterpiece

The evolutionary dance has given rise to an astonishing array of life forms, from the tiniest microorganisms to the majestic creatures roaming the savannas. Biodiversity, the result of millions of years of evolution, is nature's masterpiece. It ensures the resilience of ecosystems, providing stability and vitality to the intricate web of life. Each species, no matter how small or seemingly insignificant, contributes uniquely to the tapestry of biodiversity, enriching the planet's biological heritage.

1.19 Humanity's Dance in the Evolutionary Tapestry

In the grand evolutionary dance, humanity has taken centre stage. Through our capacity for innovation, culture, and language, we have become the architects of our environment. However, this newfound ability comes with profound responsibilities. As stewards of the Earth, we are entrusted with preserving the delicate balance of life. Our actions, from conservation efforts to sustainable practices, influence the evolutionary trajectories of countless species. It is within our power to ensure that the evolutionary dance continues for generations to come.

1.20 The Dance of Collaboration and Cooperation

While competition is a fundamental aspect of evolution, so is cooperation. The dance of evolution has seen partnerships between species, from the pollination collaborations between flowers and bees to the symbiotic relationships between animals and microbes. These partnerships illustrate the beauty of collaboration in the natural world, showing us that the dance of evolution is not just about struggle but also about harmonious cooperation.

1.21 A Symphony of Change and Continuity

The evolutionary dance is a symphony of change and continuity, a testament to the ceaseless creativity of life. It reminds us of our interconnectedness with all living beings and our shared journey through time. As we marvel at the wonders of the natural world, let us embrace our role as participants in the dance of evolution, respecting the rhythms of change and nurturing the delicate balance of life on Earth. In this dance, we find not only our origins but also our future, intricately woven into the evolutionary fabric of existence.

1.22 The Human Experience

For humans, life is a deeply personal and subjective experience. It encompasses our thoughts, emotions, relationships, and aspirations. We are not just biological beings; we are also cultural, social, and spiritual creatures. Our ability to think, reason, and reflect on our own existence sets us apart from other species.

Human life is marked by milestones such as birth, childhood, adolescence, adulthood, and old age. It is a journey filled with both joys and challenges. Our quest for meaning and purpose often leads us to explore philosophical and existential questions about the nature of life, its origins, and its ultimate meaning.

At the heart of our existence lies the profound tapestry of the human experience. It is a journey marked by a myriad of emotions, connections, challenges, and moments of immense beauty. From the exhilarating highs to the challenging lows, the human experience encapsulates the essence of what it means to be alive, to feel, to love, and to learn. Let's delve into this intricate and multifaceted journey that defines us all.

1.23 Emotions: The Colour Palette of Life

Emotions are the vibrant hues that paint the canvas of the human experience. From the warmth of love and the joy of laughter to the depths of sorrow and the pangs of fear, our emotions guide us through life's twists and turns. These feelings are not just chemical reactions but the very core of our humanity. They provide us with the capacity to empathize, to connect, and to understand the world and each other in ways unique to our species.

1.24 Connection: Threads that Bind Us Together

One of the most profound aspects of the human experience is our ability to connect with others. Whether it's the bond between parent and child, the camaraderie among friends, or the intimacy between romantic partners, these connections enrich our lives immeasurably. Through relationships, we find support in times of need, share in moments of joy, and learn the invaluable lessons of empathy and compassion. It is through these connections that we realize the depth of our shared human experience.

1.25 Challenges: Catalysts for Growth

Life is not without its challenges. In fact, it is often these hurdles that shape us the most. Each obstacle, whether personal, professional, or societal, offers an opportunity for growth and resilience. It is in facing adversity that we discover our inner strength, perseverance, and the capacity to overcome. The human experience teaches us that challenges are not roadblocks but rather stepping stones on the path to self-discovery and personal development.

1.26 Learning: The Continuous Evolution of the Self

A fundamental aspect of the human experience is the process of learning. From our first steps as infants to the wisdom acquired in old age, we are constantly evolving. We learn from our experiences, from the stories of others, and from the world around us. This continuous process of learning shapes our beliefs, perspectives, and understanding of the world. It enables us to adapt, to innovate, and to contribute meaningfully to the society we inhabit.

1.27 Creativity: Expressing the Human Soul

Creativity is the soul's way of expressing itself. Through art, music, literature, and various forms of innovation, humans have the remarkable ability to create something out of nothing. Creativity is not just about producing masterpieces; it is about finding novel solutions to problems, thinking outside the box, and exploring the uncharted realms of imagination. It is a testament to the boundless potential of the human mind and spirit.

In essence, the human experience is a profound and multifaceted journey. It is about embracing the spectrum of emotions, forging connections with others, overcoming challenges, learning and growing, and expressing the depths of our souls through creativity. As we navigate this intricate journey, let us cherish every moment, savor every emotion, and celebrate the shared human experience that unites us all. It is through our collective stories, struggles, and triumphs that the rich tapestry of the human experience is woven, reminding us of the beauty and resilience of the human spirit.

1.28 Philosophical Reflections

Philosophy, often regarded as the mother of all disciplines, is the timeless pursuit of wisdom and understanding. It delves into the fundamental questions of existence, knowledge, ethics, and reality. Philosophical reflections serve as the compass guiding humanity through the intricate maze of life, helping us make sense of the profound complexities that surround us. In this chapter, we embark on a journey into the world of philosophical contemplation, exploring its significance and the transformative power it holds.

Life has been a subject of philosophical contemplation for millennia. Philosophers, theologians, and thinkers from diverse traditions have grappled with questions about the nature of life, consciousness, and the human condition. What is the meaning of life? Is life inherently purposeful, or is it a canvas upon which we must paint our own meaning?

Existentialists like Jean-Paul Sartre have argued that life is inherently devoid of meaning, and it is up to each individual to create their own purpose. Others, like Albert Camus, have explored the inherent absurdity of life and the human struggle to find meaning in a seemingly indifferent universe.

1.29 The Quest for Meaning: Philosophy and Existential Inquiry

At the core of philosophical reflections lies the quest for meaning. Philosophers grapple with questions that have intrigued humanity for centuries: What is the meaning of life? How do we define truth? What is the nature of reality? Through rigorous inquiry and contemplation, philosophers seek to unravel the mysteries of existence, offering diverse perspectives that challenge our beliefs and expand our understanding of the world.

1.30 The Nature of Knowledge: Epistemology and the Pursuit of Truth

Epistemology, the branch of philosophy dedicated to the study of knowledge, explores questions related to belief, truth, and justification. Philosophers in this field ponder over how we acquire knowledge, the limits of human understanding, and the nature of reality. These reflections not only shape our scientific endeavours but also influence how we perceive the world around us, inviting us to critically examine our beliefs and biases.

1.31 Ethics and Morality: The Philosophical Foundations of Right and Wrong

Ethics, a cornerstone of philosophy, explores questions concerning morality, virtue, and ethical principles. Philosophical reflections in this domain prompt us to consider what is morally right or wrong, just or unjust. By examining ethical theories such as utilitarianism, deontology, and virtue ethics, we gain insights into the principles that guide human behaviour and moral decision-making, fostering a more compassionate and just society.

1.32 Metaphysics: Exploring the Nature of Reality

Metaphysics delves into the fundamental nature of reality, exploring concepts such as existence, causality, time, and identity. Philosophers in this field ponder questions about the nature of the self, the existence of free will, and the relationship between mind and body. These reflections challenge our perceptions of reality, prompting us to contemplate the nature of our existence and the underlying fabric of the universe.

1.33 The Power of Critical Thinking: Philosophy and Everyday Life

Philosophical reflections empower us with critical thinking skills essential for navigating the complexities of the modern world. By honing our ability to analyse arguments, question assumptions, and evaluate evidence, philosophy equips us to make informed decisions, engage in meaningful discourse, and challenge prevailing societal norms. It encourages us to approach issues with an open mind, fostering a culture of intellectual curiosity and respectful debate.

1.34 Philosophy and the Human Experience: A Symbiotic Relationship

In essence, philosophical reflections are intricately woven into the fabric of the human experience. They challenge our perspectives, broaden our horizons, and invite us to explore the depths of human thought and imagination. As we engage in philosophical contemplation, we embark on a transformative journey, gaining profound insights into the nature of reality, the human condition, and the moral principles that guide our actions.

In a world often filled with uncertainty and ambiguity, philosophical reflections provide us with a guiding light—a beacon of intellectual rigor and introspection. They remind us of the boundless potential of the human mind and the enduring quest for wisdom that unites us all. As we continue to ponder the philosophical questions that have captivated the greatest minds throughout history, we embark on a perpetual journey of discovery, embracing the challenges and wonders of philosophical inquiry, and enriching our understanding of ourselves and the world we inhabit.

Conclusion

Life is a multifaceted phenomenon that defies easy definition. It encompasses the biological, the personal, and the philosophical dimensions of existence. It is a story of evolution, adaptation, and diversity, and it is also a journey of self-discovery and introspection.

As we navigate the complexities of our own lives, it is worth pausing to contemplate the profound mystery of life itself. Whether we approach it from a scientific, personal, or philosophical perspective, life remains a subject of endless fascination and inquiry. It is a tapestry woven with threads of biology, experience, and meaning, and it is a story that continues to unfold with each passing moment.

CHAPTER – 2

Life Itself a Journey

Introduction

Life, the most extraordinary and unpredictable journey, weaves a tapestry of experiences, emotions, and lessons that shape our existence. From the moment of our birth to the inevitable embrace of mortality, life takes us on a remarkable odyssey, filled with moments of joy, sorrow, triumph, and heartache. In this intricate journey, we discover not only the world around us but also the depths of our own souls. Let's explore the profound nature of life as an ever-unfolding expedition of discovery, challenges, and growth.

2.1 The Journey of Self-Discovery

Life begins as a blank canvas, waiting to be painted with the colors of our experiences. As we navigate through childhood, adolescence, and into adulthood, we embark on a journey of self-discovery. We learn about our passions, fears, strengths, and weaknesses. Through relationships, achievements, and failures, we peel back the layers of our identity, uncovering the essence of who we are. This process of self-discovery is not linear; it's a continuous evolution that accompanies us throughout our lives.

2.2 Challenges: Stepping Stones to Resilience

Every journey is marked by challenges. Life, in its infinite wisdom, tests our resilience and determination through various trials. These challenges, whether in the form of personal struggles, setbacks, or adversities, are not roadblocks but stepping stones. They teach us invaluable lessons about strength, perseverance, and the depths of our capabilities. Embracing challenges transforms us, forging our character and instilling in us the courage to face the unknown.

2.3 Relationships: The Heartbeat of Life's Journey

One of the most profound aspects of life's journey is the relationships we cultivate along the way. From family and friends to romantic partners and mentors, relationships form the emotional backbone of our existence. They provide comfort in times of despair, share in our moments of happiness, and offer a sense of belonging. Through these connections, we learn the importance of love, empathy, and the joy of shared experiences. Relationships enrich our journey, adding depth and meaning to our lives.

2.4 Growth: The Essence of the Journey

Life's journey is not merely a passage of time; it is a process of continuous growth and transformation. We evolve emotionally, intellectually, and spiritually, gaining wisdom from our experiences and the knowledge acquired along the way. Growth involves embracing change, learning from mistakes, and being open to new perspectives. It is the essence of the journey, a testament to the resilience of the human spirit and the boundless potential within each of us.

2.5 Embracing the Unknown: The Adventure of a Lifetime

Life's journey is akin to an adventure into the unknown. None of us know the twists and turns that await us on the path ahead. Yet, it is precisely this uncertainty that makes the journey so exhilarating. Embracing the unknown with curiosity and courage, we embark on a quest for knowledge, fulfillment, and purpose. Each day becomes an opportunity to explore, learn, and contribute to the world in our unique way.

In conclusion, life itself is a journey—a magnificent expedition that offers us the chance to explore the depths of our humanity. It is a canvas upon which we paint our dreams, a challenge that tests our mettle, and a classroom where we learn the profound lessons of existence. As we navigate through the highs and lows, let us cherish every moment, for in the tapestry of life, it is the journey itself that holds the most profound significance, reminding us of the beauty of the human experience.

2.6 The Journey of Discovery: Navigating the Uncharted Territories of Knowledge and Self

Discovery, the very essence of human curiosity and ingenuity, fuels our desire to explore the unknown and unravel the mysteries of the world and ourselves. It is a journey that transcends physical boundaries, delving into the realms of science, philosophy, art, and personal introspection. The path of discovery is an exhilarating expedition, often marked by challenges and triumphs, leading us to the profound realization that the pursuit of knowledge is a continuous and transformative adventure.

2.7 Unveiling the Secrets of the Universe: Scientific Exploration

Scientific discovery lies at the heart of our understanding of the universe. From the microscopic world of quantum physics to the vast expanse of galaxies, scientists embark on a relentless pursuit of knowledge. The journey of scientific discovery involves meticulous observation, experimentation, and the formulation of theories that challenge existing paradigms. Through this process, humanity has uncovered the laws of nature, developed life-saving technologies, and gained insights into the origins of the cosmos, expanding our comprehension of the world in unimaginable ways.

2.8 The Creative Odyssey: Artistic Expression and Imagination

Artistic discovery is a profound exploration of human expression and creativity. Artists, musicians, writers, and creators of all kinds embark on a journey into the depths of imagination, channeling their emotions and ideas into tangible forms. Through art, we discover new perspectives, challenge societal norms, and evoke profound emotions. Artistic endeavors not only enrich our cultural heritage but also serve as a mirror reflecting the human condition, sparking conversations and encouraging introspection.

2.9 The Philosophical Quest: Exploring the Nature of Reality and Existence

Philosophical discovery delves into the fundamental questions that shape our understanding of reality, morality, and existence. Philosophers embark on a profound introspective journey, questioning the nature of truth, exploring ethical dilemmas, and pondering the mysteries of consciousness. The philosophical quest challenges us to confront our beliefs, biases, and assumptions, encouraging critical thinking and fostering a deeper understanding of the complexities of the human experience.

2.10 Self-Discovery: The Inner Journey of Personal Growth

The journey of discovery extends inward, encompassing the exploration of the self. Through introspection, mindfulness, and self-reflection, individuals embark on a transformative journey of self-discovery. This inner exploration involves understanding one's values, beliefs, strengths, and limitations. It requires confronting fears, embracing vulnerabilities, and cultivating self-compassion. The journey of self-discovery leads to personal growth, self-acceptance, and a deeper connection with one's authentic identity.

2.11 The Endless Quest: Embracing the Unknown

The journey of discovery is characterized by its endless nature. There will always be uncharted territories, both in the external world and within ourselves. Embracing the unknown with curiosity and an open mind fuels the spirit of exploration. It encourages us to ask questions, seek answers, and challenge the status quo. In the face of uncertainty, the journey of discovery becomes a testament to human resilience, determination, and the insatiable thirst for knowledge.

In conclusion, the journey of discovery is a multifaceted expedition that shapes the very fabric of human progress and understanding. It is a testament to the insatiable curiosity of the human mind and the boundless potential within each of us. As we navigate the uncharted territories of knowledge and self, let us embrace the challenges, celebrate the triumphs, and cherish the transformative power of discovery. For in the pursuit of knowledge and understanding, we embark on a journey that not only enriches our lives but also contributes to the collective wisdom of humanity, shaping the future for generations to come.

Life, as we traverse its unpredictable terrain, is not just a series of moments but a profound classroom. In this ever-changing landscape, we encounter a multitude of experiences, each laden with valuable lessons waiting to be embraced. These lessons, often disguised as challenges or moments of bliss, are the building blocks of wisdom, shaping our character and guiding us toward a more meaningful existence. As we navigate the labyrinth of life, it's crucial to recognize and cherish the lessons strewn along the way, for they hold the power to transform us.

2.12 Embracing Resilience in Adversity

Life's journey is peppered with adversities. Challenges, setbacks, and failures are not roadblocks but rather opportunities for growth. The ability to bounce back, to find strength in the face of adversity, is a vital lesson that life imparts. Every fall teaches us the art of rising, stronger and more resilient. Through adversity, we learn patience, fortitude, and the importance of tenacity.

2.13 The Value of Empathy and Kindness

One of the most profound lessons life offers is the significance of empathy and kindness. Every person we meet is fighting a battle we might know nothing about. A simple act of kindness, a compassionate gesture, has the power to brighten someone's day, and in the process, it nourishes our own soul. Life teaches us that in spreading kindness, we create ripples of positivity that reverberate far beyond our immediate actions.

2.14 Embracing Change and Adaptability

Change is the only constant in life. It teaches us to be adaptable, to adjust our sails when the winds of change blow our way. Life's lessons often come in the form of transitions, reminding us that growth lies outside our comfort zones. Embracing change allows us to evolve, learn, and discover new facets of ourselves.

2.15 The Power of Gratitude

Amidst life's challenges, there is always something to be grateful for. Gratitude is not just a virtue but a profound life lesson. It shifts our focus from what's lacking to what's abundant in our lives. By acknowledging the blessings, no matter how small, we cultivate a positive outlook, leading to a more fulfilling and content existence.

2.16 The Importance of Self-Compassion

In our journey of self-improvement, we often forget the importance of self-compassion. Life teaches us that it's okay to make mistakes, to fall short, and to have flaws. Self-compassion is about treating ourselves with the same kindness and understanding that we would offer a dear friend. It's a vital lesson that nurtures self-love and acceptance.

2.17 The Joy of Living in the Present Moment

Life's most beautiful moments are often fleeting, and they pass us by if we're too busy worrying about the future or regretting the past. The lesson of living in the present moment teaches us to savor life's experiences, to be mindful, and to find joy in the simple pleasures. It reminds us that life is happening right now, and it's up to us to fully participate in it.

2.18 The Gift of Learning and Growth

Life is a continual process of learning. Every experience, every encounter, is an opportunity to learn and grow. The wisdom acquired along the way shapes our perspectives, enriches our understanding, and refines our character. Embracing the lesson of continuous learning keeps our minds sharp and our hearts open, fostering a spirit of curiosity and enlightenment.

In essence, life's journey is an intricate tapestry woven with invaluable lessons. Each experience, whether joyful or challenging, offers an opportunity to learn and evolve. Embracing these lessons with humility and gratitude enriches our lives, transforming us into wiser, more compassionate beings. As we navigate the twists and turns of life, let's recognize the profound teachings it imparts and carry these lessons with us, for they are the treasures that illuminate our path and enrich the very fabric of our existence.

2.19 The Destinations We Seek: Journeys Beyond the Horizon

Human existence is inherently nomadic; our souls yearn for exploration, our minds thirst for new experiences, and our hearts beat with the excitement of the unknown. Life, in its essence, is a series of journeys, each one leading us towards destinations both tangible and metaphorical. These destinations represent our dreams, our aspirations, and the profound yearning to uncover the mysteries of the world and ourselves. Let's embark on a contemplative journey, exploring the diverse destinations we seek and the transformative power they hold.

2.20 Geographical Explorations: Seeking the Wonders of the World

From the mesmerizing auroras of the Arctic to the vibrant jungles of the Amazon, the world is a treasure trove of geographical marvels waiting to be discovered. We seek destinations that awe us, that challenge our perceptions, and that broaden our understanding of the planet we call home. These explorations cultivate a sense of wonder and reverence for the natural world, reminding us of the breathtaking beauty that exists beyond the confines of our everyday lives.

2.21 Intellectual Pursuits: The Quest for Knowledge

The thirst for knowledge propels us towards destinations of intellectual significance. Whether it's a prestigious university, a renowned research center, or the pages of a classic novel, our intellectual pursuits lead us towards enlightenment. The destinations of learning and wisdom empower us to think critically, to question the status quo, and to contribute meaningfully to the collective knowledge of humanity.

2.22 Creative Endeavours: The Pathways of Artistry and Expression

Creative destinations beckon the artists, musicians, writers, and innovators within us. From the stroke of a paintbrush to the melody of a song, these destinations are where imagination takes flight. They represent the boundless realms of creativity, where ideas manifest into tangible forms, inspiring awe and admiration. Creative pursuits not only enrich our lives but also illuminate the world with the brilliance of human ingenuity.

2.23 Emotional Sanctuaries: Seeking Love, Connection, and Belonging

In the tapestry of human experiences, emotional destinations hold a special place. Love, friendship, and the warmth of human connection are the emotional sanctuaries we seek. These destinations provide solace in times of distress, joy in moments of celebration, and the profound sense of belonging that makes life's journey worthwhile. The pursuit of emotional fulfillment guides us towards relationships that nourish our souls and offer unwavering support.

2.24 Spiritual Awakening: The Quest for Inner Peace and Enlightenment

The spiritual destinations we seek are often the most profound and transformative. Whether it's through meditation, prayer, or introspective practices, the quest for spiritual enlightenment leads us towards the depths of our own souls. These destinations are where we confront existential questions, find inner peace, and experience a profound sense of oneness with the universe. Spiritual pursuits provide the compass that guides us on our moral and ethical journey, shaping our beliefs and values.

In our relentless pursuit of these destinations, we uncover not just the physical landscapes but the intricate landscapes of our own hearts and minds. The destinations we seek are not merely endpoints; they are the milestones that mark our personal growth, our intellectual evolution, and our emotional resilience. They represent the facets of life that give it meaning, purpose, and a sense of fulfillment.

As we embark on these journeys, let's remember that the destinations we seek are not fixed points but evolving concepts, changing as we change, growing as we grow. Each destination is not just a place on a map but a chapter in the story of our lives, inviting us to embrace the adventure, savor the moments, and cherish the transformative power of the journeys we undertake.

2.25 The Transformative Power of the Journey: A Pathway to Self-Discovery and Growth

Life is a journey, an expedition through time and experiences that shape our existence in profound ways. Beyond the physical transitions from one place to another, the journey carries with it a transformative power that goes far deeper than miles traveled. Each step, every challenge faced, and every encounter along the way has the potential to reshape our perspectives, enrich our souls, and mold us into the individuals we are meant to be. It is in the journey, not the destination, that we find the true essence of transformation and self-discovery.

2.26 Embracing Change and Adaptability

Journeys are synonymous with change, forcing us out of our comfort zones and into the realm of the unknown. Whether it's a literal journey across continents or an emotional expedition through life's challenges, every journey demand adaptability. It is in adapting to new environments, cultures, and circumstances that we learn the art of resilience. Our ability to adjust and grow in the face of change is a testament to the transformative power of the journey.

2.27 Learning Through Challenges

Challenges and obstacles are inevitable companions on any journey. They test our mettle, pushing us beyond our limits and forcing us to confront our fears and uncertainties. In these moments of trial, we discover our inner strength, resilience, and problem-solving abilities. Every challenge becomes an opportunity for growth, teaching us invaluable lessons that shape our character and fortify our spirits. Through adversity, we not only learn about the world but also about ourselves.

2.28 Cultivating Empathy and Understanding

Journeys often lead us to encounter diverse cultures, beliefs, and ways of life. These interactions foster empathy and understanding, breaking down the barriers that divide us. By immersing ourselves in the lives and experiences of others, we broaden our perspectives, challenge our biases, and cultivate compassion. The transformative power of empathy lies in its ability to bridge gaps, fostering a sense of shared humanity that transcends geographical and cultural boundaries.

2.29 The Exploration of Self

Perhaps the most profound aspect of the journey is its ability to facilitate self-discovery. In the solitude of long walks, the serenity of nature, or the reflective moments during a solo trip, we confront our innermost thoughts and emotions. These moments of introspection allow us to understand our desires, fears, and aspirations. The journey becomes a mirror, reflecting our true selves back to us, prompting us to embrace our strengths and acknowledge our weaknesses. Through this self-exploration, we embark on a transformative process of personal growth and self-acceptance.

2.30 Fostering Gratitude and Mindfulness

Journeys, especially those that take us to new places, have a way of instilling a deep sense of gratitude. Gratitude for the experiences, the people we meet, and the beauty of the world around us. It encourages us to be mindful, to live in the present moment, and to appreciate the small wonders of life. The journey teaches us that every sunset, every shared laugh, and every moment of quiet contemplation is a precious gift, encouraging us to approach life with gratitude and mindfulness.

The transformative power of the journey lies not just in the physical distance covered but in the emotional and spiritual milestones achieved. It is a catalyst for self-discovery, personal growth, and a deeper understanding of the world and our place in it. As we embark on the various journeys that life presents, let us embrace the challenges, savor the lessons, and acknowledge the profound impact these experiences have on our lives. Through the transformative power of the journey, we become not only travellers of the world but explorers of our own souls, discovering the depths of our resilience, compassion, and inner strength.

Life itself is a journey—a profound odyssey of discovery, growth, and transformation. It is a voyage through the unknown, marked by lessons, destinations, and the enduring power to shape who we become. As we navigate the twists and turns of existence, let us embrace the journey with an open heart and a curious spirit, for it is in the journey itself that we find the true essence of life

CHAPTER – 3

Visualizing Beyond Gender

Introduction

In today's rapidly evolving world, conversations surrounding gender have become more nuanced and inclusive than ever before. Traditional binary views of gender are gradually giving way to a more complex understanding, acknowledging a diverse spectrum of identities that extend far beyond the confines of male and female. As society becomes more accepting and aware, it is crucial to explore and celebrate the visual representation of gender diversity. This chapter delves into the importance of visualizing beyond gender and how it fosters a more inclusive and understanding society.

3.1 Breaking the Binary

Historically, society has often viewed gender through a binary lens – male or female. However, this simplistic perspective fails to encompass the rich tapestry of human identity. Non-binary, genderqueer, genderfluid, agender, and many other identities challenge the traditional norms, highlighting that gender is not a fixed concept but a fluid spectrum.

Visual representation plays a pivotal role in dismantling these outdated norms. Artists, photographers, and filmmakers are increasingly embracing diverse gender identities in their work, depicting the beautiful complexity of human experiences. These representations not only empower individuals to embrace their authentic selves but also educate society about the existence and validity of non-binary identities.

3.2 The Power of Media

Media, in all its forms, wields immense influence over public perceptions. Television shows, movies, advertisements, and social media platforms have the power to shape societal attitudes. By incorporating characters and stories that reflect a broad range of gender identities, media can challenge stereotypes and broaden the horizons of public understanding.

Furthermore, social media platforms have become a powerful tool for individuals to express their gender identities authentically. Platforms like Instagram, TikTok, and YouTube provide a space for non-binary individuals to share their stories, experiences, and art, fostering a sense of community and belonging.

3.3 Education and Awareness

Education is a cornerstone in the journey towards a more inclusive society. Schools and educational institutions must incorporate comprehensive sex education that includes discussions about diverse gender identities. By teaching young people about the spectrum of gender, we can foster empathy, understanding, and acceptance from an early age.

Moreover, public awareness campaigns can play a crucial role in challenging stereotypes and promoting inclusivity. These campaigns can feature diverse gender identities, showcasing the beauty of human variation and reinforcing the message that everyone deserves respect and acceptance, regardless of their gender identity.

3.4 Intersectionality and Inclusivity

It is essential to recognize that gender identity does not exist in isolation; it intersects with various other aspects of a person's identity, such as race, ethnicity, sexual orientation, and socioeconomic background. Embracing intersectionality ensures that the experiences of individuals with diverse gender identities are understood within the context of their entire identity, fostering a more nuanced and empathetic understanding. Visualizing beyond gender is not just a matter of representation; it is a powerful catalyst for social change. By embracing and celebrating the diverse spectrum of gender identities, we can create a more inclusive society where everyone is valued and respected for who they are. Through education, media representation, and awareness campaigns, we can challenge existing norms and pave the way for a future where gender diversity is not just acknowledged but celebrated as an essential part of the human experience.

3.5 The Spectrum of Gender: Embracing Diversity and Inclusion

In recent years, society has made significant strides in understanding and acknowledging that gender is far more complex than the traditional binary concept of male and female. The recognition of gender as a spectrum has opened up new avenues for discussions, challenging stereotypes, and fostering inclusivity. This chapter explores the spectrum of gender, emphasizing the importance of acceptance, respect, and celebration of diverse gender identities.

3.6 Understanding the Spectrum

The gender spectrum is a framework that recognizes the infinite diversity of human gender experiences. At one end of the spectrum are individuals who identify strictly with the gender assigned to them at birth, commonly referred to as cisgender. At the other end are individuals who identify with a gender different from the one assigned to them, known as transgender. In between these points lie a multitude of identities, including non-binary, genderqueer, genderfluid, agender, bigender, and more. Each of these identities represents a unique way in which individuals experience and express their gender.

3.7 Breaking Free from Binary Constraints

The acknowledgment of the gender spectrum dismantles the rigid societal norms that have confined individuals within the binary constraints of male and female. By embracing the spectrum, society allows individuals the freedom to explore their gender identity without fear of judgment or discrimination. This acceptance is not just a matter of tolerance but an active celebration of the rich tapestry of human experiences.

3.8 Challenging Stereotypes and Prejudices

One of the most significant benefits of understanding the gender spectrum is its potential to challenge stereotypes and prejudices. Stereotypes related to gender have far-reaching consequences, affecting how individuals are perceived, treated, and even how they perceive themselves. By recognizing the diversity of gender identities, society can combat harmful stereotypes and promote a more inclusive environment where everyone is valued for their authentic selves.

3.9 Supporting Mental and Emotional Well-being

Acceptance and understanding of diverse gender identities are essential for the mental and emotional well-being of individuals. When people feel seen, respected, and accepted for who they are, it can significantly improve their self-esteem and mental health. Creating a supportive environment where individuals can express their gender identity without fear of discrimination can lead to greater overall well-being and a stronger sense of community.

3.10 Promoting Inclusivity in Education and Workplaces

Educational institutions and workplaces play a crucial role in promoting inclusivity. By incorporating comprehensive education about gender diversity, schools can nurture empathy and understanding among students, paving the way for a more accepting society. In workplaces, policies that protect gender diversity and create safe spaces for individuals of all gender identities are essential. Inclusive workplaces not only foster a positive work environment but also boost productivity and creativity by embracing diverse perspectives.

Understanding the spectrum of gender is a journey toward a more compassionate and inclusive world. By challenging traditional norms, stereotypes, and prejudices, society can create a space where every individual, regardless of their gender identity, is valued and respected. Embracing the diversity of gender identities enriches the human experience, fostering empathy, acceptance, and love. As we continue to learn and grow, let us celebrate the spectrum of gender and work towards a future where everyone is free to be their authentic selves without fear or discrimination.

3.11 Challenging Gender Stereotypes: Breaking the Chains of Tradition

Gender stereotypes have long plagued societies, imposing rigid expectations on individuals based on their assigned gender at birth. These stereotypes limit personal expression, perpetuate inequality, and stifle the potential of countless people. However, in the wake of a more enlightened era, it is essential to challenge these stereotypes actively. This chapter delves into the importance of challenging gender stereotypes and how doing so can pave the way for a more inclusive, diverse, and equal world.

3.12 The Pervasiveness of Gender Stereotypes

Gender stereotypes are deeply ingrained in cultures worldwide, dictating how individuals should behave, dress, and pursue their ambitions. Men are often expected to be strong, unemotional, and assertive, while women are encouraged to be nurturing, passive, and accommodating. These stereotypes not only limit the choices and opportunities available to individuals but also reinforce harmful power imbalances.

3.13 Breaking the Mold: Empowering Women

Challenging gender stereotypes is paramount in empowering women. It means recognizing and supporting women's choices, whether it's pursuing careers in male-dominated fields, opting for leadership roles, or choosing unconventional paths. Empowering women involves providing equal access to education, ensuring reproductive rights, and eliminating workplace discrimination, enabling them to break free from societal constraints.

3.14 Redefining Masculinity: Freeing Men from Expectations

Men, too, suffer under the weight of gender stereotypes. The expectation to be stoic and unyielding emotionally can lead to mental health issues and strain relationships. Challenging stereotypes allows men to express vulnerability, seek help when needed, and redefine masculinity beyond aggression and dominance. Embracing emotional intelligence and empathy enables men to build healthier relationships and contribute positively to their communities.

3.15 Fostering Inclusivity for Non-Binary and Genderqueer Individuals

Gender stereotypes not only marginalize cisgender individuals but also pose significant challenges for non-binary, genderqueer, and gender-nonconforming people. Challenging these stereotypes involves recognizing and respecting diverse gender identities. Creating inclusive spaces where individuals can express their gender identity freely is essential, whether it's in education, healthcare, or the workplace. Pronoun awareness and gender-neutral facilities are small steps that make a significant difference.

3.16 Education as a Catalyst for Change

Education plays a pivotal role in challenging gender stereotypes. By incorporating diverse narratives and role models in curricula, schools can teach children that gender is not a determinant of ability or worth. Comprehensive sex education that includes discussions about consent, gender identity, and sexual orientation can foster understanding and acceptance from an early age, breaking the cycle of stereotypes perpetuated through generations.

3.17 Media's Responsibility and Impact

Media has a powerful influence on shaping societal attitudes. By portraying diverse gender roles and breaking stereotypes in movies, television shows, advertisements, and literature, media can challenge traditional norms. Responsible media representation not only reflects the reality of diverse identities but also shapes public perceptions, dismantling harmful stereotypes and fostering acceptance. Challenging gender stereotypes is not just a social obligation but a moral imperative. Embracing diverse gender identities and breaking free from the confines of traditional roles can create a world where everyone, regardless of their gender, can thrive. By actively challenging these stereotypes in our communities, workplaces, and educational institutions, we can create a future where individuals are free to express themselves authentically, unencumbered by the chains of tradition. Together, let us build a world where gender stereotypes are but a relic of the past, replaced by a celebration of the rich tapestry of human identity.

3.18 Media and Representation: Shaping Narratives, Breaking Stereotypes

Media holds a mirror to society, reflecting its values, norms, and aspirations. In this digital age, where information travels at the speed of light, the role of media in shaping public perceptions is more significant than ever. Representation in media, encompassing diverse gender identities, cultures, abilities, and backgrounds, has the power to challenge prejudices, break stereotypes, and foster a more inclusive society. This chapter explores the profound impact of media representation and the responsibility it bears in shaping narratives that promote diversity and acceptance.

3.19 The Power of Visibility

Representation in media goes beyond mere visibility; it validates experiences and identities. When individuals from marginalized communities see themselves accurately portrayed in movies, TV shows, advertisements, and news outlets, it fosters a sense of belonging and acceptance. Moreover, it educates the wider public, bridging the gap of understanding and empathy between different social groups.

3.20 Breaking Stereotypes and Challenging Norms

Media has the transformative ability to challenge stereotypes and norms deeply entrenched in society. By portraying characters who defy traditional gender roles, challenge racial biases, or overcome disabilities, media can reshape public attitudes. When these narratives are woven into the fabric of popular culture, they influence social perceptions, gradually breaking down prejudices and fostering acceptance.

3.21 Fostering Empathy and Understanding

Well-crafted stories humanize diverse experiences, allowing audiences to empathize with characters irrespective of their backgrounds. By showcasing the struggles, joys, and aspirations of individuals from different walks of life, media engenders understanding. It prompts viewers to walk in the shoes of others, cultivating empathy and dismantling preconceived notions.

3.22 The Responsibility of Media

Media outlets, content creators, and filmmakers carry a significant responsibility. They are the architects of societal narratives, and their choices influence public opinion. It is crucial for media professionals to be aware of the impact their work has on shaping attitudes. Responsible representation involves authenticity, avoiding harmful stereotypes, and actively including diverse voices in the creative process. Sensitivity and research are key, ensuring that narratives are respectful, accurate, and nuanced.

3.23 Encouraging Diversity Behind the Scenes

True representation not only involves diverse characters on-screen but also extends to the talent behind the scenes. Promoting diversity among writers, directors, producers, and executives ensures a broader range of perspectives. When people from different backgrounds are involved in decision-making processes, it enriches storytelling, making narratives more authentic and relatable.

Media and representation are inseparable elements of our modern society. The narratives we consume influence our perceptions, attitudes, and, ultimately, our actions. By embracing diverse voices, challenging stereotypes, and fostering empathy, media can be a powerful force for positive change. It has the potential to inspire, educate, and unite people across cultures and identities.

As consumers of media, it is essential to be discerning, supporting content that celebrates diversity and challenges biases. By recognizing the influence of media on our collective mindset, we can encourage a media landscape that truly reflects the rich mosaic of humanity, fostering understanding, acceptance, and unity in an increasingly interconnected world.

3.24 Inclusivity in Design and Marketing: Celebrating Diversity, Fostering Connection

In the rapidly evolving global landscape, where diversity is the cornerstone of vibrant societies, businesses and designers must recognize the significance of inclusivity. Inclusivity in design and marketing not only reflects the diverse tapestry of humanity but also fosters a sense of belonging, understanding, and connection. This chapter explores the importance of embracing inclusivity in design and marketing strategies, emphasizing the positive impact it has on both businesses and the communities they serve.

3.25 Designing for Diversity

Inclusive design is the practice of creating products, spaces, and experiences that consider the full range of human diversity. It involves designing with empathy, ensuring that everyone, regardless of age, ability, gender, or cultural background, can access and engage with a product or service seamlessly. This approach not only broadens the customer base but also enhances user experience, making products and services more accessible and user-friendly for everyone.

3.26 Representation in Marketing

Representation in marketing is a powerful tool that can shape societal norms and perceptions. When marketing campaigns feature diverse individuals – different races, ethnicities, body types, gender identities, and abilities – it sends a strong message of inclusivity. Consumers, especially those from underrepresented communities, feel seen and valued, building a strong emotional connection with the brand. Moreover, diverse representation challenges stereotypes and promotes a more inclusive and accepting society.

3.27 Cultural Competence and Sensitivity

In our interconnected world, businesses often operate on a global scale. Understanding and respecting cultural differences are fundamental to inclusive marketing. Cultural competence involves being aware of, respecting, and integrating diverse cultural practices and traditions into marketing strategies. It ensures that campaigns are not only sensitive but also resonate deeply with diverse audiences, establishing trust and credibility.

3.28 Accessible Design for All

Inclusive design extends to digital platforms. Websites, mobile apps, and online content should be accessible to individuals with disabilities. This includes using alt text for images, ensuring keyboard navigation, and providing captions for videos. A website that is accessible to everyone not only adheres to legal requirements but also demonstrates a commitment to inclusivity, opening doors for a wider audience and potential customers.

3.29 The Business Benefits of Inclusivity

Embracing inclusivity is not just a moral imperative; it makes good business sense. Companies that prioritize diversity and inclusivity are more innovative and better positioned to meet the needs of a diverse customer base. Inclusivity fosters creativity within teams, leading to fresh ideas and perspectives. Moreover, it enhances brand reputation, attracting socially conscious consumers who appreciate and support businesses that align with their values. Inclusivity in design and marketing is not a trend; it is an ethical responsibility and a business necessity. Embracing diversity in all its forms enriches the creative process, fosters empathy, and strengthens connections between businesses and their audiences. As consumers become more discerning and socially aware, companies that champion inclusivity will not only thrive economically but also contribute significantly to building a more inclusive, understanding, and harmonious world. By celebrating diversity in design and marketing, businesses have the power to shape a future where everyone is recognized, respected, and valued.

3.30 Education and Awareness: Catalysts for a Better Tomorrow

Education and awareness are the cornerstones of progress, enlightenment, and societal development. They empower individuals, communities, and nations, enabling them to break free from ignorance, prejudice, and inequality. In this interconnected world, where information flows seamlessly, education and awareness play pivotal roles in shaping informed citizens, fostering inclusivity, and driving positive change. This chapter explores the transformative power of education and awareness, highlighting their profound impact on individuals and societies.

3.31 Empowering Minds and Hearts

Education is not merely the acquisition of knowledge; it is the key to unlocking human potential. Through education, individuals gain critical thinking skills, knowledge about the world, and the ability to navigate complex challenges. Moreover, education nurtures empathy, tolerance, and understanding, shaping compassionate individuals who contribute positively to society. Informed citizens are better equipped to engage in meaningful dialogue, challenge prejudices, and work towards building harmonious communities.

3.32 Education as a Tool for Social Equity

Access to quality education is a fundamental human right that can bridge the gap between privilege and poverty. Education empowers marginalized communities, providing them with opportunities for socio-economic advancement. By ensuring equal access to education for all, regardless of gender, race, or socio-economic background, societies can break the cycle of poverty and empower generations to come. Education becomes a transformative force, enabling individuals to escape the confines of their circumstances and aspire for a better future.

3.33 Raising Awareness: Igniting Social Change

Awareness campaigns serve as powerful tools for addressing social issues, promoting health, and advocating for change. Whether it's raising awareness about environmental conservation, mental health, gender equality, or social justice, these campaigns educate the public, challenge prejudices, and inspire action. Through the use of various media platforms, awareness campaigns have the potential to reach millions, sparking conversations and mobilizing communities to work collectively towards common goals.

3.34 Technology and Global Awareness

In the digital age, technology has amplified the reach of education and awareness initiatives. Online platforms, social media, podcasts, and webinars provide accessible channels for disseminating information and promoting awareness. Technology enables global collaboration, allowing individuals from different corners of the world to share knowledge, experiences, and solutions. Online education platforms make learning accessible to individuals who might otherwise lack educational opportunities, breaking down barriers and fostering a global community of learners.

3.35 Education and Awareness for Sustainable Development

Education and awareness are essential components of sustainable development. Educating communities about sustainable practices, environmental conservation, and responsible consumption can mitigate the adverse effects of climate change. Informed citizens are more likely to adopt eco-friendly habits and support policies that prioritize environmental protection. Moreover, awareness campaigns about sustainable development goals can inspire individuals, businesses, and governments to work collaboratively towards creating a more sustainable future for all. Education and awareness are not just processes; they are transformative journeys that elevate individuals and societies to new heights. By investing in education and promoting awareness, societies can break barriers, challenge stereotypes, and foster a culture of understanding and acceptance. Informed individuals are the architects of progress, capable of building a world where knowledge is a beacon of hope, ignorance is dispelled, and compassion reigns supreme. As we invest in education and awareness, we pave the way for a brighter, more equitable, and harmonious future for generations to come.

3.36 Conclusion

Visualizing beyond gender is a journey toward a more inclusive and accepting world. It involves recognizing the diversity of gender experiences, challenging harmful stereotypes, and creating spaces and representations that are inclusive of all gender identities. As we continue on this path, we move closer to a society where everyone is free to express themselves authentically, regardless of the constraints of traditional gender norms. In embracing this journey, we celebrate the richness of human diversity and the potential for a more equitable and compassionate future.**Top of Form**

CHAPTER – 4

Realizing Soul

The concept of the soul has intrigued and inspired humanity for centuries. Across cultures and belief systems, the soul represents an enigmatic essence that transcends the physical body and connects us to something greater. In this chapter, we embark on a journey to explore the idea of realizing the soul—what it means, how it is perceived in various traditions, and the profound impact it can have on one's life. The concept of the soul has fascinated humanity for millennia. Across cultures, religions, and philosophies, the idea of an eternal, inner essence that defines our truest self has been a source of profound contemplation. In the hustle and bustle of modern life, the pursuit of material goals often overshadows the exploration of our innermost being.

4.1 The Soul: Beyond the Physical Realm

In various spiritual traditions, the soul is considered the eternal, unchanging core of a person. It's often described as the seat of consciousness, the source of inner peace, and the connection to a higher, universal consciousness. Unlike the physical body, which is transient, the soul is believed to be eternal and beyond the confines of time and space. Realizing the soul involves transcending the material world and delving into the depths of one's consciousness.

4.2 The Journey Inward: Self-Reflection and Meditation

Realizing the soul necessitates introspection and self-reflection. Taking time for contemplation, meditation, or mindfulness practices allows individuals to quiet the mind and connect with their inner selves. Through meditation, people often report profound spiritual experiences, a sense of unity with the universe, and a deep understanding of their purpose in life. Regular practice can lead to a heightened sense of awareness, increased empathy, and a profound sense of inner peace.

4.3 Transcending Ego: Letting Go of Illusions

The ego, or the sense of individual identity, often creates a barrier to realizing the soul. Ego-driven desires, fears, and attachments cloud the clarity of our true nature. Realizing the soul involves transcending the ego, letting go of illusions of separateness, and understanding the interconnectedness of all living beings. This shift in perspective fosters a sense of unity, compassion, and love for all creation.

4.4 Service to Others: A Path to Soul Realization

Many spiritual traditions emphasize the importance of service to others as a means to realize the soul. Acts of kindness, compassion, and selflessness not only benefit others but also cultivate qualities such as humility and empathy within the individual. By serving others, individuals can experience the interconnectedness of all life and recognize the divine spark within every being.

4.5 Beyond Religious Boundaries: Universal Soul Realization

The concept of realizing the soul is not confined to any particular religion or belief system. It is a universal pursuit that transcends religious boundaries. People from diverse spiritual backgrounds, or even those without any religious affiliation, can embark on the journey of soul realization. It is a deeply personal quest that can be pursued through various spiritual practices, philosophical inquiry, or even scientific exploration of consciousness.

4.6 The Infinite Journey Within

Realizing the soul is a profound and infinite journey that leads to self-discovery, inner peace, and a sense of purpose. It is a transformative experience that can enrich every aspect of life, fostering a deep sense of interconnectedness with all living beings and the universe at large. As individuals embark on this inner journey, they not only discover the eternal essence within themselves but also contribute to creating a more compassionate and harmonious world for all. The realization of the soul, therefore, is not just a personal achievement but a gift to humanity, illuminating the path toward a more enlightened existence.

4.7 The Soul Across Cultures: A Tapestry of Beliefs and Understanding

The concept of the soul is a thread that weaves through the fabric of human history and culture. Across civilizations, continents, and centuries, the idea of an eternal, immaterial essence that defines our true nature has shaped religious beliefs, philosophical doctrines, and cultural practices. This chapter explores the diverse and fascinating interpretations of the soul across cultures, emphasizing the universal themes that connect humanity's spiritual understanding.

4.8 Ancient Roots: The Soul in Early Civilizations

From ancient Egyptian beliefs in the afterlife to the Hindu concept of Atman, the soul has been a central tenet in early civilizations. In Egyptian mythology, the soul, or 'ka,' was thought to continue its journey after death. In Hinduism, the soul, Atman, is considered eternal and divine, connecting every living being with the cosmic consciousness. Similarly, ancient Greek philosophy introduced the idea of an immortal soul, distinguishing it from the physical body, paving the way for Western philosophical thought.

4.9 Abrahamic Faiths: Soul and Divine Connection

In the Abrahamic religions – Judaism, Christianity, and Islam – the soul is regarded as a divine creation, intimately linked with the concept of God. In these traditions, the soul is believed to be a unique, eternal essence that undergoes judgment after death, determining one's fate in the afterlife. The understanding of the soul's purpose and its connection to the divine is central to the moral and ethical teachings in these faiths.

4.10 Eastern Philosophies: Soul and Reincarnation

Eastern religions and philosophies, such as Buddhism and Jainism, introduce the idea of reincarnation, where the soul undergoes a cycle of birth, death, and rebirth (samsara). The soul's karma, or accumulated actions, determines its future existence. In these traditions, the ultimate goal often lies in liberating the soul from this cycle, achieving enlightenment, and merging with the universal consciousness.

4.11 Indigenous Beliefs: Soul and Ancestral Connection

Indigenous cultures around the world have diverse beliefs about the soul and its connection to nature and ancestors. Many indigenous societies believe that the soul is not only within individuals but also permeates the natural world. Ancestral spirits are often revered and considered essential parts of the community's collective soul, fostering a deep sense of interconnectedness between the living, the deceased, and nature.

4.12 Modern Perspectives: Psychology and the Soul

In contemporary times, the concept of the soul has also found resonance in psychological and spiritual discourse. Depth psychology, particularly in the works of Carl Jung, delves into the notion of the soul as the unconscious, the deeper, hidden aspects of the human psyche. Integrative and transpersonal psychology explore the soul's connection to spirituality, emphasizing self-discovery, inner healing, and the pursuit of a meaningful life.

4.13 Unity in Diversity

The varied interpretations of the soul across cultures illustrate the richness of human spirituality and the diverse paths humanity takes in its quest for understanding. While the specifics may differ, the universal themes of interconnectedness, transcendence, and the pursuit of a higher purpose bind these beliefs together. As we explore the myriad interpretations of the soul across cultures, we find not only diversity but also unity – a shared human longing to comprehend the profound mystery of our existence and the essence that defines us all. Top of Form

4.14 Self-Exploration and Inner Journey: Navigating the Depths of the Soul

In the hustle and bustle of modern life, amid the cacophony of external influences, the art of self-exploration and inner journey often takes a back seat. However, delving into the depths of our own consciousness, understanding our emotions, thoughts, and beliefs, and embarking on an inner journey, is a transformative and enlightening process. This chapter explores the profound significance of self-exploration and the inner journey, emphasizing their impact on personal growth, mental well-being, and the pursuit of a meaningful life.

4.15 The Call Within: Understanding the Need for Self-Exploration

The journey of self-exploration begins with a deep introspection, a willingness to question our beliefs and biases, and a curiosity to explore the intricacies of our inner world. It is a quest to understand the essence of who we are beyond the roles we play in society – a son, daughter, professional, or friend. Recognizing this inner call is the first step towards embarking on a transformative voyage.

4.16 The Path of Self-Discovery: Unraveling Layers of Identity

Self-exploration involves peeling off layers of societal conditioning, fears, and insecurities to discover the authentic self. It is about embracing vulnerability, acknowledging strengths and weaknesses, and accepting imperfections. Through practices like journaling, meditation, or therapy, individuals can unravel suppressed emotions, confront past traumas, and cultivate self-compassion, leading to a profound sense of self-awareness and acceptance.

4.17 Embracing Mindfulness: Being Present in the Moment

The practice of mindfulness is an integral part of the inner journey. By being fully present in the moment, individuals can observe their thoughts and emotions without judgment. Mindfulness fosters self-awareness, allowing individuals to recognize recurring patterns of thought and behavior. This awareness provides the foundation for positive change, helping individuals respond to situations consciously, rather than reacting impulsively.

4.18 The Role of Challenges: Growth Through Adversity

Challenges and adversities often serve as catalysts for self-exploration. Difficulties in life prompt individuals to question their beliefs, values, and priorities. Facing challenges head-on, with self-reflection and resilience, can lead to profound personal growth. Adversity becomes an opportunity for inner strength to emerge, enabling individuals to navigate life's complexities with grace and wisdom.

4.19 Connecting with Spirituality: A Deeper Understanding of Self

Many individuals find solace and guidance in spiritual practices during their inner journey. Whether through meditation, prayer, or contemplation, connecting with spirituality provides a sense of purpose and a deeper understanding of the self. It fosters a sense of interconnectedness with the universe, offering profound insights into the mysteries of existence and one's place in the grand tapestry of life.

4.20 The Endless Odyssey Within

Self-exploration and the inner journey are not destinations but continuous processes of growth and self-discovery. As individuals delve into the depths of their souls, they embark on an odyssey that leads to greater self-awareness, empathy, and a profound sense of inner peace. The journey within is not always easy; it requires courage, patience, and self-compassion. However, the rewards – a deeper understanding of oneself, meaningful relationships, and a sense of purpose – make this journey one of the most enriching experiences of a lifetime. Embracing the path of self-exploration is not just a choice; it is a transformative commitment to living a life of authenticity, fulfillment, and profound wisdom.

4.21 Transcending Ego: The Pathway to Spiritual Awakening

The ego, often perceived as the voice in our heads that narrates our life story, is an essential aspect of our identity. However, spiritual traditions worldwide emphasize the need to transcend the ego to achieve a deeper understanding of life and experience spiritual enlightenment. This chapter explores the concept of transcending ego, shedding light on its significance in various philosophical and spiritual contexts and how it leads to profound personal transformation.

4.22 Understanding the Ego

The ego, in psychological terms, is the conscious mind, responsible for our sense of self and individuality. While it plays a crucial role in our daily lives, it can also create barriers, limiting our perception of reality. Ego-driven thoughts and desires often lead to attachments, fear, and a distorted view of the world.

4.23 Transcending Ego in Eastern Philosophies

In Eastern philosophies such as Buddhism and Hinduism, transcending ego is central to achieving spiritual liberation. Buddhism teaches that attachment and desire, fueled by the ego, lead to suffering. By letting go of attachments and realizing the impermanent nature of all things, individuals can attain Nirvana, a state of ultimate enlightenment and freedom from the cycle of suffering.

Similarly, in Hinduism, the ego, known as the 'ahamkara,' creates a false sense of individuality. Through practices like meditation and self-realization, individuals can realize their true nature, the Atman, which is beyond the ego. This realization leads to Moksha, liberation from the cycle of birth and death.

4.24 Transcending Ego in Western Philosophies

In Western philosophical traditions, thinkers like Friedrich Nietzsche and Søren Kierkegaard explored the concept of transcending ego. Nietzsche believed that individuals could overcome the limitations of the ego by embracing their 'will to power,' a driving force that pushes them beyond their perceived boundaries. Kierkegaard emphasized the importance of faith and the acceptance of uncertainty, transcending the ego's need for absolute knowledge and control.

4.25 Practical Approaches to Transcending Ego

1. **Mindfulness and Meditation:** Mindfulness practices cultivate awareness of ego-driven thoughts and emotions. Through meditation, individuals can observe these thoughts without judgment, leading to a sense of detachment and a broader perspective.
2. **Practicing Gratitude:** Gratitude shifts the focus from ego-driven desires to appreciating the present moment and acknowledging the interconnectedness of all life.

3. **Service to Others:** Engaging in selfless acts of kindness and service diminishes the ego's dominance, fostering a sense of unity and compassion for others.
4. **Self-Reflection:** Regular self-reflection encourages individuals to question their beliefs, motivations, and desires, leading to a deeper understanding of the ego's influence on their lives.

4.26 Liberation Beyond the Self

Transcending ego is a transformative journey that leads to liberation from the constraints of self-centeredness. By understanding the ego's limitations and embracing practices that foster self-awareness and compassion, individuals can experience profound spiritual growth. The journey to transcend the ego is not a denial of the self but a profound realization that true freedom lies in transcending the boundaries of the individual self and connecting with the vast, interconnected web of existence. Through this liberation, individuals find not only inner peace but also a deep sense of unity with the universe, paving the way for spiritual awakening and profound enlightenment.

4.27 Connection with the Divine: Nurturing the Soul's Spiritual Journey

The concept of a connection with the divine is a fundamental aspect of human spirituality. Across cultures, religions, and belief systems, people have sought to establish a link with a higher power, the transcendent, or the divine. This profound connection serves as a guiding light, offering solace, purpose, and a deeper understanding of the mysteries of life. This chapter explores the significance of establishing a connection with the divine, delving into its transformative power and the ways in which it enriches the human experience.Top of Form

4.28 The Universal Longing

Throughout history, humans have experienced a deep yearning to connect with something greater than themselves. Whether it's the monotheistic worship of God in Abrahamic religions, the interconnectedness with nature in indigenous belief systems, or the pursuit of enlightenment in Eastern philosophies, the desire to establish a connection with the divine transcends cultural boundaries. This universal longing reflects humanity's innate spiritual nature and the search for meaning and purpose in life.

4.29 Finding Meaning and Purpose

For many, the connection with the divine provides a profound sense of purpose and meaning. Belief in a higher power often offers a moral and ethical framework, guiding individuals in their actions and decisions. It provides comfort in times of hardship, offering solace and hope. Through prayer, rituals, and spiritual practices, individuals seek divine guidance, finding direction and clarity in the face of life's challenges.

4.30 Nurturing Inner Peace and Tranquility

Establishing a connection with the divine can lead to inner peace and tranquility. Many spiritual traditions emphasize the importance of contemplation, meditation, and prayer as ways to quiet the mind and connect with the divine presence within and around us. In moments of stillness, individuals often experience a sense of unity, serenity, and a deep inner calm, transcending the stresses of everyday life.

4.31 Fostering Compassion and Love

The connection with the divine is often associated with qualities such as love, compassion, and forgiveness. Many religious teachings emphasize the importance of loving one's neighbors, showing kindness to others, and practicing forgiveness. Through the divine connection, individuals are inspired to cultivate these virtues, fostering harmonious relationships, social cohesion, and a sense of unity among diverse communities.

4.32 A Source of Creativity and Inspiration

Art, music, literature, and various forms of creative expression have often been inspired by the connection with the divine. Many artists, poets, and musicians attribute their creativity and inspiration to a higher power. This connection serves as a wellspring of artistic expression, allowing individuals to channel divine energies into their creative works, enriching the cultural tapestry of humanity.

4.33 A Profound Spiritual Journey

The connection with the divine is a deeply personal and transformative journey. It provides a sense of belonging to something greater, nurturing the soul, and offering guidance and purpose in life. Regardless of religious or cultural differences, this universal connection serves as a unifying force, reminding humanity of its shared spiritual heritage. In the pursuit of this connection, individuals find not only solace and meaning but also a profound sense of unity with the divine and with one another, enriching the human experience and fostering a deeper understanding of the interconnectedness of all life.

4.34 Realization of soul

Realizing the soul is a journey of self-discovery and spiritual awakening that transcends cultural, religious, and philosophical boundaries. It is an exploration of the innermost essence of our being, a quest to connect with the divine, and a path to self-realization. In a world often focused on external pursuits, understanding and realizing the soul can bring profound meaning and fulfillment to one's life, leading to a deeper understanding of the self and the universe. It is a journey worth embarking upon for those seeking purpose, inner peace, and a connection to something greater than themselves.

CHAPTER – 5

Understanding Life After Life

Introduction

The question of what happens after death has been a subject of profound contemplation and speculation across cultures and religions. The concept of life after life, or the continuation of existence beyond the physical body, has inspired spiritual traditions, philosophical inquiries, and artistic expressions throughout human history. This chapter delves into the diverse beliefs and perspectives surrounding life after life, exploring the enigmatic journey of the soul and the profound mysteries that lie beyond mortality.

5.1 Reincarnation: The Cycle of Existence

One of the most prevalent concepts related to life after life is reincarnation. Found in religions such as Hinduism, Buddhism, and certain New Age beliefs, reincarnation posits that the soul undergoes a cycle of birth, death, and rebirth. The experiences and actions in each life shape the soul's evolution, guiding it towards spiritual enlightenment or liberation from the cycle of reincarnation. This belief offers a perspective where life is a continuous journey of learning and growth, transcending the boundaries of individual lifetimes.

5.2 Heaven and Hell: The Dichotomy of Destinies

In many religious traditions, such as Christianity, Islam, and Judaism, the concept of an afterlife includes the notions of heaven and hell. Heaven is often described as a realm of eternal bliss, where righteous souls experience divine communion and fulfillment. Conversely, hell is depicted as a realm of punishment, where the souls of the unrighteous face torment and suffering. These beliefs serve as moral compasses, encouraging virtuous living to secure a place in the paradisiacal afterlife.

5.3 Near-Death Experiences: Glimpses Beyond the Veil

Near-death experiences (NDEs) have been reported by individuals who have faced imminent death and then revived. These experiences often include vivid sensations of leaving the body, moving through a tunnel, encountering deceased loved ones, and entering a realm of light and unconditional love. While scientific explanations exist, NDEs are frequently interpreted as glimpses into the afterlife, providing a glimpse of what might await beyond the threshold of mortality.

5.4 The Journey of the Soul: Mystical and Esoteric Perspectives

Mystical traditions across various religions offer unique insights into the journey of the soul after death. These traditions, including Kabbalah in Judaism, Sufism in Islam, and Gnosticism in Christianity, explore the esoteric dimensions of existence. They often posit that the soul's journey involves ascending through spiritual realms, attaining higher states of consciousness, and ultimately merging with the divine source. Such beliefs underline the interconnectedness of all souls and their ultimate reunion with the divine.

5.5 The Endless Quest for Understanding

While the question of life after life remains shrouded in mystery, it continues to captivate the human imagination and fuel the quest for spiritual understanding. Whether through religious teachings, near-death experiences, or mystical insights, humanity's fascination with the afterlife reflects a deeper yearning for meaning, transcendence, and the eternal nature of the soul. As individuals explore these diverse perspectives, they engage in a profound contemplation of existence itself, embracing the mystery and embracing the journey with a sense of wonder, humility, and reverence for the unknown.

5.6 Diverse Beliefs About the Afterlife: Navigating the Spiritual Landscape

The afterlife, a realm beyond the mortal existence, has been a topic of fascination, fear, and profound curiosity for humans throughout history. Across cultures, religions, and belief systems, diverse perspectives on what happens after death have emerged, reflecting the complexity of the human imagination and the deeply rooted spiritual questions about existence and beyond. This chapter explores the multifaceted tapestry of beliefs surrounding the afterlife, highlighting the rich diversity in human understanding and interpretation.

The belief in life after life varies greatly among cultures and religions. Here are a few examples:

1. **Reincarnation**: In Hinduism and Buddhism, the concept of reincarnation is central. It holds that the soul is reborn into a new body after death, based on the karmic consequences of one's actions in previous lives. Reincarnation offers the potential for spiritual growth over multiple lifetimes.
2. **Heaven and Hell:** In many Abrahamic religions such as Christianity, Islam, and Judaism, the afterlife is often conceived as a binary existence: heaven, a realm of eternal bliss and communion with the divine, and hell, a place of punishment and separation from God. The concept of an afterlife serves as a moral compass, shaping ethical behavior and inspiring faith through the promise of divine reward and the threat of divine retribution.
3. **Spiritual Continuation**: Some belief systems, including various New Age and indigenous spiritual practices, emphasize the idea of spiritual continuation. They suggest that the soul or

consciousness endures in a non-physical form, perhaps as a spirit guide or an energy presence.

4. **Atheistic Views:** Atheists and secular humanists, who do not subscribe to religious beliefs, often contend that there is no afterlife. From their perspective, life is finite, and death is the cessation of consciousness.
5. **Reincarnation: Eastern Philosophies** In contrast to the Abrahamic traditions, many Eastern philosophies such as Hinduism, Buddhism, and Jainism embrace the concept of reincarnation. According to this belief, the soul undergoes a cycle of rebirth, each life influenced by past actions (karma). Reincarnation provides a framework for spiritual evolution, allowing individuals to learn and grow across multiple lifetimes until they achieve enlightenment or liberation from the cycle of rebirth.
6. **Ancestral Spirits: Indigenous Beliefs** Numerous indigenous cultures around the world hold unique beliefs about the afterlife, often centered around ancestral spirits. In these traditions, the departed continue to exist in the spiritual realm, remaining connected to the living. Rituals and ceremonies are performed to honor and communicate with these spirits, seeking guidance, protection, and blessings. Ancestral beliefs underline the enduring bond between generations and the reciprocal relationship between the living and the deceased.
7. **Nirvana and Enlightenment:** Buddhism offers a distinctive perspective on the afterlife. The ultimate goal in Buddhism is to attain Nirvana, a state of liberation from suffering and the cycle of rebirth. Achieving Nirvana involves transcending desires, attachments, and the ego, leading to a state of profound enlightenment and spiritual liberation. Buddhists believe that by following the Eightfold Path and cultivating mindfulness,

individuals can escape the cycle of samsara (rebirth) and attain Nirvana.

8. **Spiritual Realms and Reunion: New Age and Spiritualist Beliefs** In New Age and Spiritualist movements, diverse beliefs about the afterlife abound. Some envision a realm of spiritual growth and learning, where souls reunite with loved ones and continue their evolutionary journey. Others explore the possibility of communication with spirits through mediums, emphasizing the continuity of consciousness beyond physical death. These beliefs often emphasize love, healing, and the interconnectedness of all souls.

5.7 Embracing the Diversity of Belief

The myriad beliefs about the afterlife reflect humanity's deep-seated spiritual yearning and the quest for understanding the mysteries of existence. While these beliefs may differ widely, they share a common thread: the recognition of life's profound spiritual dimensions. Embracing the diversity of afterlife beliefs invites a deeper appreciation for the rich tapestry of human spirituality, fostering tolerance, respect, and a sense of wonder about the enigmatic journey that awaits beyond this life. As individuals navigate these diverse beliefs, they engage in a collective exploration of the eternal questions about life, death, and the boundless realms of the human spirit.

5.8 Philosophical Perspectives on Life After Life: Exploring the Eternal Questions of Existence

Philosophy, the discipline that seeks to unravel the fundamental questions of human existence, has long grappled with the concept of life after life. Philosophers, through the ages, have delved deep into metaphysical realms, contemplating the nature of consciousness, the soul, and the possibility of an existence beyond the mortal coil. This chapter explores the diverse and profound philosophical perspectives on life after life, shedding light on the intricate tapestry of thought that surrounds this eternal question.

5.9 Dualism: Mind and Body

One of the foundational philosophical concepts regarding life after life is dualism, famously championed by René Descartes. Dualism posits that the mind (or soul) and the body are distinct entities. While the body perishes, the soul, being non-physical, can persist beyond death. This perspective offers the possibility of an afterlife, where the soul continues its existence in a realm beyond the material world, providing a foundation for various religious beliefs about the immortal nature of consciousness.

5.10 Materialism: The End of Consciousness

Materialist philosophies, in contrast, reject the notion of an afterlife. Influenced by scientific discoveries, materialism posits that consciousness is a product of physical processes within the brain. From this perspective, when the body ceases to function, consciousness, too, comes to an end. Materialism challenges the existence of an immortal soul, grounding the concept of life after life in the realm of human imagination rather than objective reality.

5.11 Eternal Recurrence: Cyclical Existence

Friedrich Nietzsche proposed the concept of eternal recurrence, suggesting that the universe and all events within it are eternally recurring in an infinite cycle. In this view, life after life is not a continuation of the individual soul but a repetition of the entire universe, including our lives, in perpetuity. This philosophical perspective challenges traditional notions of linear time and questions the significance of individual existence in the grand scheme of eternal recurrence.

5.12 Existentialism: Creating Meaning in the Absence of Afterlife

Existentialist philosophers like Jean-Paul Sartre and Albert Camus grapple with the idea of life's meaning in the absence of an afterlife. Existentialism emphasizes individual freedom and responsibility, positing that humans must create their own purpose and meaning in a seemingly indifferent universe. In this perspective, the absence of an afterlife heightens the significance of the present life, urging individuals to embrace existence fully and authentically.

5.13 Cosmic Consciousness: Unity with the Universe

Some philosophical traditions explore the concept of cosmic consciousness, suggesting that individual consciousness is interconnected with the larger cosmic or universal consciousness. From this perspective, life after life transcends the boundaries of individual existence, merging with the universal consciousness. This perspective offers a mystical interpretation of existence, emphasizing unity, interconnectedness, and the eternal nature of consciousness.

5.14 The Endless Quest for Understanding

Philosophical perspectives on life after life reflect the profound depth of human inquiry into existence, mortality, and the nature of consciousness. As philosophers continue to contemplate these fundamental questions, diverse and often contradictory perspectives emerge, each offering a unique lens through which to view the mysteries of life beyond death. Ultimately, the philosophical exploration of life after life serves as a testament to the boundless curiosity of the human spirit, inviting contemplation, discussion, and a deeper understanding of the enigmatic journey that awaits beyond the threshold of mortality.

5.15 Scientific Inquiries and Near-Death Experiences

Near-death experiences (NDEs) have been reported by individuals who have come close to death and returned with vivid accounts of profound and often mystical experiences. These narratives often involve feelings of peace, seeing a bright light, encountering deceased loved ones, and sometimes, traveling through a tunnel. While these experiences are deeply personal and often spiritually transformative, they also raise intriguing questions for scientific inquiry. This chapter explores the intersection between scientific investigations and near-death experiences, delving into the attempts to understand these mystical encounters through the lens of empirical research and rational inquiry.

5.16 The Nature of Near-Death Experiences

Near-death experiences have been documented across cultures and belief systems, sharing common elements such as the sensation of floating, seeing one's body from an out-of-body perspective, and encountering a sense of love and warmth. These experiences often challenge conventional scientific explanations, as they involve perceptions and consciousness when the brain is believed to be non-functional.

5.17 Scientific Investigations and Neurological Correlates

Scientists have sought to understand the biological and neurological basis of near-death experiences. Some researchers propose that these experiences are the result of specific patterns of brain activity, such as the release of neurotransmitters or oxygen deprivation. Studies using neuroimaging techniques have explored the brain regions associated with NDEs, attempting to identify the neural correlates of these extraordinary experiences.

5.18 Out-of-Body Experiences and Consciousness

Out-of-body experiences (OBEs), a common element of near-death experiences, have been a subject of scientific interest. Some scientists suggest that OBEs could be linked to disturbances in the brain's multisensory integration processes, leading to a disconnection between sensory input and one's sense of body ownership. Research in this area explores the relationship between consciousness, perception, and the brain, shedding light on the complex nature of human awareness.

5.19 Transcendental and Mystical Elements

Many near-death experiences involve encounters with a divine presence, spiritual beings, or a profound sense of interconnectedness with the universe. These mystical elements challenge the materialistic worldview of mainstream science. Some researchers explore the parallels between NDEs and mystical experiences induced by psychedelics or meditation, examining the common themes of ego dissolution, unity, and a sense of the infinite.

5.20 The Role of Consciousness in Near-Death Experiences

Consciousness, a fundamental aspect of human existence, remains one of the most intriguing and debated topics in both philosophy and science. Near-death experiences, with their transcendental and mystical qualities, provide a unique window into the nature of consciousness. Scientists explore the possibility that consciousness may exist independently of the brain, challenging traditional materialistic perspectives and opening the door to new philosophical inquiries about the nature of reality.

5.21 A Multifaceted Exploration

The intersection between scientific inquiries and near-death experiences represents a complex and multifaceted exploration of human consciousness and the nature of reality. While science strives to understand these mystical encounters through empirical methods, the profound and transformative nature of near-death experiences challenges the boundaries of our current scientific understanding. As research in this area continues, it not only sheds light on the enigmatic realm of NDEs but also invites a broader philosophical inquiry into the interconnectedness of the material and the mystical, bridging the gap between the scientific and the spiritual in the quest for a deeper understanding of the human experience.

The concept of life after life is a deeply ingrained and complex aspect of human existence. It encompasses diverse beliefs, philosophical perspectives, and scientific inquiries. Whether one embraces a religious view, contemplates the mysteries of consciousness, or seeks empirical evidence through scientific study, the question of what, if anything, lies beyond death continues to captivate our collective imagination. Ultimately, the exploration of life after life reflects our enduring quest for meaning, understanding, and the eternal nature of the human spirit

CHAPTER – 6

Journey After Life – Truth Revealed

6.1 Introduction

The concept of what happens after death has been a profound mystery that has fascinated humanity for centuries. Various religions, spiritual traditions, and philosophical schools of thought offer diverse interpretations of the journey after life. In this chapter, we will embark on a deep exploration, seeking to uncover the truths, beliefs, and mysteries surrounding the afterlife and the journey beyond mortal existence.

6.2 Exploring Religious Perspectives

Different religions offer unique and intricate narratives about the afterlife. Christianity presents the concepts of heaven and hell, emphasizing moral conduct and divine judgment. Islam describes an afterlife where individuals are accountable for their deeds, determining their fate in paradise or hell. Hinduism and Buddhism propose the cyclical nature of existence, involving reincarnation and the pursuit of enlightenment.

6.3 Mystical and Near-Death Experiences

Mystical traditions, meditation practices, and near-death experiences (NDEs) offer intriguing glimpses into the afterlife. Many mystics across traditions describe a union with the divine, a merging of the individual soul with the cosmic consciousness. NDEs, often reported by individuals who have been revived after being clinically dead, describe experiences of light, peace, and encounters with deceased loved ones, challenging scientific explanations and pointing towards a life beyond the physical realm.

6.4 Philosophical Inquiries into Life After Death

Philosophers have pondered the concept of an afterlife for centuries. Dualism suggests the separation of the soul from the body, allowing for the existence of consciousness beyond death. Materialism, on the other hand, asserts that consciousness ceases to exist when the body dies. Existentialism delves into the human experience, emphasizing the significance of life in the absence of an afterlife, focusing on individual freedom and creating meaning in the present.

6.5 Scientific Exploration of Consciousness

In recent years, scientific inquiries into consciousness have sparked intriguing debates about the possibility of an afterlife. Quantum physics explores the interconnectedness of all things, raising questions about the nature of consciousness and its potential continuity beyond death. Neuroscientific studies delve into near-death experiences, exploring the brain's activity during these profound moments, attempting to decipher the mysteries of the mind and consciousness.

6.6 Cultural and Folk Beliefs

Cultures around the world possess rich and diverse beliefs about the afterlife. From ancient Egyptian beliefs in the journey through the underworld to the Norse concept of Valhalla, where warriors go after death, these cultural narratives provide unique perspectives on the post-mortal journey. Folk beliefs, too, often involve notions of spirits, reincarnation, and ancestral realms, emphasizing the continuity of existence beyond physical death.

6.7 Embracing the Mystery

The journey after life remains one of humanity's greatest mysteries, a subject of profound fascination and contemplation. While religious traditions offer spiritual solace, mystical experiences provide glimpses into the transcendental, and scientific inquiries shed light on the nature of consciousness, the ultimate truth remains elusive. As we explore the diverse beliefs and perspectives on the afterlife, we are reminded of the deep human need to understand the enigmatic journey that awaits us all. Embracing the mystery of the journey after life invites a sense of wonder, humility, and reverence for the profound and eternal questions that continue to shape the human experience.

6.8 Philosophical Contemplations on the Journey After Life: Exploring the Infinite Horizon of Existence

The nature of existence after death has been a perennial subject of philosophical contemplation. Philosophers, ancient and contemporary alike, have delved into the metaphysical realms, pondering the essence of the soul, the possibility of an afterlife, and the eternal journey beyond mortal boundaries. This chapter delves into the philosophical contemplations surrounding the journey after life, exploring the profound questions, theories, and musings that have shaped human understanding of the infinite horizon of existence.

6.9 The Immortality of the Soul: Plato and the Quest for Eternal Truth

In the ancient philosophical tradition, Plato envisioned the soul as immortal. He believed that the soul is eternal, unchanging, and belongs to the realm of Forms, transcending the physical world. According to Plato, the soul's journey after life involves returning to the realm of Forms, seeking knowledge and wisdom in its purest essence. This contemplation laid the foundation for the Western philosophical discourse on the immortality of the soul.

6.10 Karma and Reincarnation: Eastern Philosophies and the Cycle of Life

Eastern philosophies, particularly Hinduism and Buddhism, introduce the concepts of karma and reincarnation. Karma, the law of cause and effect, dictates the consequences of one's actions, influencing the course of future lives. Reincarnation, the cyclical rebirth of the soul, offers opportunities for spiritual growth and liberation (moksha/ nirvana). This philosophical perspective contemplates existence as a continuous journey of learning and enlightenment, with each life shaping the soul's evolution.

6.11 The Existential Paradox: Absurdity and the Absence of Afterlife

Existentialist philosophers such as Jean-Paul Sartre and Albert Camus grappled with the absence of inherent meaning in life. From an existential perspective, life after death is a paradox – a possibility that challenges the existential concept of individual freedom and the creation of personal meaning. Facing the possibility of a finite existence, existentialism encourages individuals to embrace life's absurdity and create their own purpose in the face of the unknown.

6.12 The Quantum Soul: Consciousness and the Infinite Possibilities

In contemporary philosophical discourse, quantum physics has sparked intriguing contemplations about the nature of consciousness and the soul. Some philosophers propose that consciousness might be quantum in nature, existing beyond the boundaries of the physical body. Quantum mechanics, with its mysterious principles like entanglement and superposition, raises questions about the interconnectedness of consciousness and the potential for an afterlife existing in a realm beyond classical physics.

6.13 Transcendental Consciousness: Eastern and Western Mysticism

Mystical traditions in both Eastern and Western philosophies explore the concept of transcendental consciousness. Mystics, through meditation, prayer, or spiritual experiences, claim to access states of consciousness that transcend the ordinary perception of reality. These contemplations suggest the possibility of the soul's journey into higher dimensions, where it merges with the divine or the universal consciousness, emphasizing the interconnectedness of all existence.

6.14 Embracing the Infinite Possibilities

Philosophical contemplations on the journey after life encompass a vast spectrum of beliefs, from the eternal nature of the soul to the existential acceptance of life's inherent uncertainty. As humans, our contemplation of life after death reflects our deepest existential fears, hopes, and curiosities. Embracing these philosophical perspectives invites us to explore the infinite possibilities, encouraging a profound dialogue about the nature of existence, consciousness, and the eternal mystery that awaits us all beyond the veil of mortality. In these contemplations, we find not only philosophical inquiry but also a celebration of the human spirit's endless quest for understanding the enigmatic journey that transcends life's physical boundaries.

The concept of the journey after life is a profound and enduring aspect of human culture and thought. It encompasses a rich tapestry of beliefs, mystical experiences, and philosophical reflections. Whether rooted in religious faith, guided by spiritual intuition, or scrutinized through the lens of reason and science, the question of what lies beyond death continues to intrigue and inspire us.

Ultimately, the journey after life remains one of the greatest mysteries of the human experience. It reflects our eternal quest for meaning, understanding, and the eternal nature of the soul or consciousness. While the truth about the afterlife may continue to elude us, the exploration of this enigma reminds us of the deep, timeless questions that define our existence.

CHAPTER – 7

Karma Formulae

7.1 Introduction

Karma is a concept deeply ingrained in various philosophies and belief systems across the world, from Hinduism and Buddhism to New Age spirituality. It embodies the idea that our actions have consequences, and these consequences shape our present and future experiences. While karma is often discussed in a mystical or spiritual context, it can also be viewed through a more practical lens as a formula that governs our actions and their repercussions. In this chapter, we will explore the concept of karma as a formula, dissecting its components and understanding its implications.

7.2 The Basics of Karma

Karma is often simplified into the adage: "You reap what you sow." At its core, it suggests that our intentions and actions have an impact on our lives, and this impact can be either positive or negative. The concept of karma is not limited to a single lifetime; it extends beyond the boundaries of time, with the effects of our actions rippling into future existences in some belief systems.

Karma, a fundamental concept in various Eastern philosophies and religions, is a term that has permeated popular culture and spiritual discourse. Often used colloquially, its deeper philosophical meaning extends far beyond mere actions and consequences. In this chapter, we will explore the basics of karma, unraveling the profound principles behind this ancient teaching and its impact on individual lives and the world at large.

7.3 Defining Karma

At its core, karma is the law of cause and effect. The word '**karma**' originates from the Sanskrit language and means '**action**' or '**deed**.' In the context of karma, it refers to the actions and intentions that shape our lives and influence our future experiences. According to the concept of karma, every action, whether physical, mental, or emotional, has consequences – positive or negative – that will manifest in this life or future lives.

7.4 The Principle of Cause and Effect

Karma operates on the principle of cause and effect, suggesting that our actions and intentions create ripples in the fabric of the universe. Positive actions lead to positive outcomes, while negative actions result in undesirable consequences. This principle emphasizes personal responsibility and accountability for one's deeds, highlighting the interconnectedness of all living beings and their shared destiny.

7.5 Types of Karma

In the realm of karma, actions are categorized into different types:

1. **Sanchita Karma:** The accumulated karma from past lives, representing the sum total of all actions and their consequences.
2. **Prarabdha Karma:** The portion of sanchita karma that is chosen to be experienced in the current lifetime, determining the circumstances and events of one's life.
3. **Kriyamana Karma:** The karma generated through current actions, shaping future experiences.
4. **Agami Karma:** The karma that will be created in the future based on present actions and intentions

7.6 Understanding Good and Bad Karma

Karma is not inherently good or bad; it is the intention behind the action that determines its moral quality. Positive actions rooted in kindness, compassion, and selflessness generate good karma, leading to favorable outcomes. Conversely, negative actions driven by greed, hatred, and harm create bad karma, resulting in unfavorable consequences. It is the intention, awareness, and mindfulness behind every action that profoundly influence the karmic outcomes.

7.7 The Role of Free Will and Destiny

Karma does not negate the concept of free will. While past actions shape our present circumstances, individuals have the power to make choices and create new karma through their intentions and actions. The law of karma emphasizes personal agency, encouraging individuals to make conscious choices aligned with positive values and ethical principles, thereby shaping their destiny.

7.8 Living Mindfully and Responsibly

Understanding the basics of karma invites individuals to live mindfully, recognizing the impact of their actions on their lives and the world. It encourages self-reflection, empathy, and ethical conduct, fostering a sense of interconnectedness and responsibility toward others and the environment. Embracing the concept of karma is not merely an abstract philosophical idea; it is a practical guide for leading a conscious and purposeful life, creating positive ripples in the vast web of existence we all share.

7.9 The Art of Intention, Action, and Consequence

Karma, the ancient concept rooted in Eastern philosophies, is not just a theoretical idea but a guiding principle for ethical living and spiritual growth. Understanding the karma formula in practice involves recognizing the intricate relationship between intention, action, and consequence. In this chapter, we will delve deeply into the practical aspects of karma, exploring how our intentions shape our actions and, in turn, influence the outcomes in our lives and the world around us.

7.10 Action (Deeds and Words)

Intentions find expression through actions, both physical and verbal. Every action we undertake, every word we speak, is a manifestation of our intentions. Acts of kindness, generosity, and empathy contribute to positive karma, fostering harmony and well-being. Conversely, actions that cause harm, deception, or suffering generate negative karma, leading to discord and imbalance. The law of karma emphasizes the importance of ethical conduct in our interactions with others and the world.

7.11 Intention (Thoughts and Desires)

At the heart of the karma formula lies intention. Our thoughts, desires, and motivations drive our actions. Intention sets the tone for the energy we emit into the world. Positive intentions rooted in kindness, compassion, and love generate good karma. Similarly, negative intentions driven by greed, envy, or hatred create bad karma. The quality of our intentions profoundly impacts the moral value of our actions.

7.12 Consequence (Outcome and Impact)

The consequences of our actions, whether immediate or delayed, form the basis of the karmic cycle. Positive actions yield favorable outcomes, such as happiness, peace, and positive relationships. Similarly, negative actions result in unfavorable consequences, such as conflict, pain, and discord. The law of karma suggests that every action, regardless of its scale, leaves an imprint on the universe, shaping the course of our lives and influencing the collective destiny of humanity.

7.13 Breaking Down the Karma Formula

To understand karma as a formula, let's break it down into its essential components

Karma as a Formula: $K = A + I + C$

Putting it all together, we can represent karma.

Karma (K) = Actions (A) + Intentions (I) + Consequences (C)

1. **Actions** (A): The first part of the karma equation is our actions. These include not only our physical deeds but also our thoughts, intentions, and emotions. Every action we take, whether conscious or unconscious, contributes to our karmic account.
2. **Intentions** (I): The motivations behind our actions play a crucial role in the karma formula. Actions driven by good intentions and compassion are believed to generate positive karma, while actions motivated by negativity or selfishness may result in negative karma.
3. **Consequences** (C): Karma involves the idea that every action sets in motion a series of consequences. These consequences are not limited to a linear cause-and-effect relationship; they can manifest in various ways and at different times. The principle of karma suggests that our actions and intentions ultimately shape the experiences we encounter in life.

Understanding the Karma Formula in Practice

1. **Positive Karma**: When our actions are rooted in kindness, empathy, and selflessness, and when our intentions are pure, positive karma is generated. This can lead to favorable consequences in our lives, such as happiness, success, and fulfilling relationships.
2. **Negative Karma**: Actions driven by negative intentions, such as harm, greed, or deceit, generate negative karma. Negative karma can result in adverse consequences, such as suffering, challenges, and obstacles.
3. **Karmic Balance**: The concept of karma also implies that the universe seeks balance. If we accumulate negative karma, it is believed that we may experience challenges or adversity to

balance the scales. Similarly, positive karma can lead to favorable circumstances.

4. **Free Will:** It's essential to note that karma is not deterministic. We have the capacity to change our actions and intentions, thereby altering the course of our karmic journey. Recognizing the power of free will allows us to actively shape our karma.

7.14 Practical Application of the Karma Formula

1. **Mindfulness and Self-awareness:** Practicing mindfulness enables us to become aware of our thoughts, emotions and intentions. By cultivating self-awareness, we can identify negative tendencies and transform them into positive intentions, fostering good karma.
2. **Compassionate Action:** Engaging in acts of kindness, compassion, and generosity promotes positive karma. Acts of service to others, without expecting anything in return, create a ripple effect of positivity and contribute to the well-being of society.
3. **Ethical Decision-making:** Making ethical choices in all aspects of life, including relationships, work, and social interactions, aligns our actions with positive intentions. Ethical conduct is the cornerstone of generating good karma and fostering harmonious relationships.
4. **Responsibility and Accountability:** Acknowledging our actions, taking responsibility for their consequences, and learning from our mistakes are essential aspects of the karma formula. By accepting accountability, we can actively work towards transforming negative patterns and generating positive outcomes.

7.15 Living Consciously and Intentionally

Understanding the karma formula in practice empowers individuals to live consciously and intentionally. By aligning our intentions with positive actions, we can shape our destiny and contribute to the collective well-being of humanity. Embracing the principles of karma fosters a sense of responsibility, compassion, and interconnectedness, guiding us towards a more harmonious existence with ourselves, others, and the world. As we navigate the complexities of life, the wisdom of karma serves as a timeless guide, reminding us of the profound impact of our intentions and actions on the intricate web of existence.

Conclusion

The concept of karma, when viewed as a formula, offers a framework for understanding the relationship between our actions, intentions, and life's consequences. It encourages us to be mindful of our choices, fostering a sense of responsibility for our actions and their impact on ourselves and the world around us. While the intricacies of karma remain a subject of spiritual and philosophical exploration, the idea that our actions matter and influence our lives is a universal and timeless truth. By embracing this understanding, we can strive to live with greater consciousness and compassion, seeking to sow the seeds of positive karma in our journey through life.

CHAPTER – 8

Equating Life Balance

In the hustle and bustle of modern life, finding equilibrium is akin to mastering an intricate equation. The variables in this equation are the various aspects of our lives—work, family, health, social connections, personal interests, and more. Striking the right balance between these elements is essential for our overall well-being and happiness. In this pursuit, we embark on a journey that involves understanding, recalibrating, and often, redefining our priorities.

Life is a complex equation, composed of various elements that require balance to achieve harmony and well-being. Just as mathematical equations rely on equal parts to yield a balanced result, our lives need equilibrium in different areas to thrive. In this chapter, we will explore the concept of equating life balance, highlighting the key components and strategies to ensure a fulfilling and harmonious existence

8.1 Understanding the Equation: The Components of Well-Being

Well-being is not a singular concept but a multifaceted one. It encompasses physical, mental, emotional, and social health. Each component is interlinked, and a disturbance in one can affect the others.

1. **Physical Health**: Exercise, nutrition, and sufficient rest are the cornerstones of physical well-being. A balanced diet, regular exercise, and adequate sleep contribute significantly to our overall health.

2. **Mental and Emotional Health**: Mental well-being involves managing stress, practicing mindfulness, and seeking help when needed. Emotional health entails understanding and managing our emotions effectively, fostering resilience, and nurturing self-compassion.
3. **Social Connections:** Human beings are inherently social creatures. Meaningful relationships, both familial and social, provide emotional support, reduce stress, and enhance our overall sense of belonging.
4. **Personal Growth:** Pursuing hobbies, learning new skills, and setting and achieving goals contribute to personal growth. It fosters a sense of accomplishment and purpose.
5. **Work-Life Balance:** Balancing professional responsibilities and personal life is crucial. It involves setting boundaries, managing time effectively, and knowing when to step back and recharge.

8.2 Recalibrating Priorities: Finding Your Balance

Finding equilibrium in life is a deeply personal journey. What works for one person may not work for another. It requires introspection, self-awareness, and the courage to make changes when necessary.

1. **Reflect on Your Values**: What matters most to you? Is it your family, your career, your health, or something else? Identifying your core values helps you align your priorities accordingly.
2. **Set Realistic Goals**: Establish achievable short-term and long-term goals in various aspects of your life. Goals provide direction and motivation, guiding you towards a more balanced life.
3. **Learn to Say No**: It's essential to recognize your limitations and not overcommit yourself. Saying no, when necessary, allows you to focus on your priorities and prevents burnout.
4. **Practice Self-Care:** Prioritize self-care activities that rejuvenate you—whether it's reading, exercising, meditating, or spending

time with loved ones. Taking care of yourself enables you to be more present and effective in other areas of your life.

5. **Seek Support:** Don't be afraid to seek support from friends, family, or professionals when needed. Asking for help is a sign of strength, not weakness.

8.3 Balancing the Equation of Life

Achieving balance in life is a dynamic and ongoing process that requires conscious effort and adaptability. Here are some strategies to help you equate the various elements of life:

1. **Prioritize Self-Care:** Self-care is not a luxury but a necessity. Make time for activities that recharge you mentally and physically, whether it's reading, meditation, or spending time in nature.
2. **Set Boundaries:** Establish clear boundaries in all areas of life, from work to relationships. Boundaries protect your well-being and prevent burnout.
3. **Practice Mindfulness:** Cultivate mindfulness through practices like meditation and deep breathing. Mindfulness helps you stay present and better manage stress.
4. **Maintain Healthy Relationships:** Invest time and effort in nurturing healthy relationships. Communication, empathy, and active listening are key to successful connections.
5. **Time Management:** Manage your time effectively by setting priorities and goals. Organize your schedule to allocate time to different aspects of your life.
6. **Seek Support:** Don't hesitate to seek support when needed. Whether it's from friends, family, or a therapist, seeking help is a sign of strength.
7. **Embrace Flexibility:** Life is dynamic, and circumstances change. Be adaptable and open to adjusting your equation of balance as needed.

8. **Reflect and Adjust**: Regularly reflect on your life balance. Assess whether certain areas are neglected or overemphasized, and make adjustments accordingly.

Life is dynamic, and so is the equation of well-being. As circumstances change—a new job, a new relationship, or a change in health—our priorities and the balance between various aspects of our lives may shift. Embracing change and being adaptable are essential in maintaining equilibrium.

1. **Embrace Flexibility**: Be open to adjusting your routines and priorities as life evolves. What worked for you in one phase of life may need adjustments in another.
2. **Practice Mindfulness**: Mindfulness, the practice of being present and fully engaged in the moment, can help you navigate through life's challenges with grace and composure.
3. **Celebrate Progress**, Not Perfection: Striving for balance doesn't mean achieving perfection in every area of your life. Celebrate your progress, no matter how small, and acknowledge that setbacks are a natural part of the journey.

In the intricate equation of well-being, the variables are numerous, and the solutions are diverse. There is no one-size-fits-all approach. Instead, it's about understanding your unique equation, recalibrating your priorities, and being open to the inevitable changes that life brings. As you navigate this equation, remember that the key lies in embracing the process, finding joy in the journey, and nurturing a sense of balance that aligns with your authentic self.

CHAPTER – 9

How to Choose Destination After Life

9.1 Introduction

The concept of an afterlife has captivated human imagination for millennia, and the idea of consciously choosing one's destination in the hereafter is a fascinating and thought-provoking notion. While religious and spiritual traditions often offer their own interpretations of the afterlife, I would likc to explore the idea of how one might begin their journey to a chosen afterlife destination, blending elements of belief, philosophy, and personal reflection.

Life, as we know it, is a fleeting moment in the grand tapestry of existence. The concept of an afterlife has fascinated and perplexed humanity for centuries. The notion that there might be something beyond the realms of our earthly existence raises profound questions about the nature of consciousness, the soul, and the ultimate purpose of our being. While this topic delves into the realms of spirituality, faith, and philosophy, the idea of choosing a destination after life sparks curiosity and contemplation. Here, we explore this metaphysical concept from various perspectives, acknowledging the diverse beliefs and interpretations that humanity holds.

9.2 Exploring Religious Beliefs

Different religions offer unique perspectives on what happens after life. For instance, in Christianity, heaven and hell are often depicted as destinations based on one's deeds and faith during their earthly life. In Hinduism and Buddhism, the concept of reincarnation suggests that one's actions in this life determine their state in the next. Understanding and aligning with the beliefs of a particular religion often influence an individual's choice of an afterlife destination.

9.3 Contemplating the Nature of Consciousness

Some philosophical and spiritual traditions propose that consciousness is not limited to the physical body. Instead, it is a universal force that transcends the boundaries of life and death. Those who resonate with such beliefs might perceive the afterlife as a merging of individual consciousness with the cosmic or divine consciousness, rather than a specific destination.

9.4 Seeking Personal Enlightenment

For many, the afterlife journey is a quest for personal growth and enlightenment. It involves transcending the ego, understanding the interconnectedness of all beings, and attaining a state of inner peace. In this view, the afterlife represents a continuation of the spiritual journey, unbound by the constraints of the physical body.

9.5 Considering Cultural and Mythological Influences

Cultural stories, myths, and legends often shape our perceptions of the afterlife. Ancient civilizations had diverse beliefs, from the Elysian Fields of Greek mythology to the Hall of Two Truths in ancient Egyptian beliefs. These cultural narratives can influence an individual's imagination and choice of an afterlife destination.

9.6 Embracing the Unknown

For some, the concept of an afterlife remains a mystery, a great unknown waiting to be explored. Embracing the mystery of what comes after life can be a source of comfort, encouraging individuals to live fully in the present moment and appreciate the beauty of existence without being overly preoccupied with what may lie ahead.

9.7 Respecting Diverse Perspectives

One of the fundamental aspects of the afterlife concept is its diversity. People across the world hold varying beliefs, and each perspective is deeply personal and meaningful to those who adhere to it. Respecting these diverse viewpoints fosters understanding, tolerance, and harmony among individuals and communities.

In the end, the choice of an afterlife destination, or even the belief in such a concept, is deeply personal. It reflects the intricate tapestry of human spirituality, shaped by culture, religion, philosophy, and personal experiences. Regardless of one's beliefs, the contemplation of life beyond its earthly bounds invites us to reflect on the essence of our existence, fostering a deeper understanding of the human spirit and the mysteries that surround it.

9.8 Understanding Afterlife Beliefs

Before embarking on the journey to a chosen afterlife destination, it's essential to understand the diversity of afterlife beliefs that exist across cultures and belief systems. These beliefs can be broadly categorized into several categories:

1. **Reincarnation**: Many Eastern religions, such as Hinduism and Buddhism, believe in the cyclical process of reincarnation. Individuals are believed to be reborn into new bodies based on their karma from previous lives.
2. **Heaven and Hell**: Monotheistic religions like Christianity, Islam, and Judaism often teach about an afterlife with heavenly and hellish realms. One's destination in the afterlife is determined by their faith and deeds during their earthly life.
3. **Spiritual Continuation**: Some belief systems, including New Age spirituality and certain indigenous traditions, emphasize spiritual continuation. They propose that the soul or consciousness endures in a non-physical form, allowing for a variety of afterlife experiences.

9.9 Reflecting on Personal Beliefs

The journey to a chosen afterlife destination begins with personal reflection and self-exploration. Here are some steps to help you navigate your beliefs and preferences:

1. **Examine Your Beliefs**: Reflect on your personal beliefs and values regarding the afterlife. Are you drawn to a specific religious or spiritual tradition, or do you resonate more with universal or eclectic beliefs?
2. **Consider Your Morality**: Evaluate your ethical and moral principles. Many afterlife beliefs are closely tied to one's actions and intentions during their earthly life. What kind of life do you aspire to lead, and how does it align with your desired afterlife destination?
3. **Seek Guidance**: Engage in discussions with spiritual mentors, leaders, or advisors who can provide insights into various afterlife beliefs. They can help you explore different paths and perspectives.
4. **Explore Inner Spirituality**: Consider engaging in practices like meditation, prayer, or self-reflection to connect with your inner spirituality. These practices can help you gain clarity about your beliefs and desires.

9.10 Taking Practical Steps

Once you have a clearer understanding of your beliefs and preferences, you can take practical steps to align your life with your chosen afterlife destination:

1. **Live Your Values:** Strive to live in accordance with your chosen beliefs and values. This may involve acts of kindness, charity, or spiritual devotion, depending on your belief system.

2. **Learn and Grow**: Continuously seek knowledge and personal growth. Many belief systems emphasize the importance of spiritual development as a means to attain a favorable afterlife.
3. **Embrace Rituals and Practices:** Engage in rituals or practices that are meaningful to your chosen path. This can include attending religious services, performing daily prayers or meditations, or participating in ceremonies.
4. **Connect with a Community**: Join or connect with a community of like-minded individuals who share your beliefs. Community support can provide guidance, encouragement, and a sense of belonging.

CHAPTER – 10

The Conclusion

10.1 Introduction

The concept of a journey after life, explored through various beliefs, philosophies, and spiritual traditions, invites us to ponder the mysteries of existence beyond our mortal coil. Throughout this series of chapter, we've delved into the diverse interpretations of the afterlife, the quest for meaning and purpose, and the pursuit of balance and harmony. In this concluding note, we reflect on the enduring significance of the journey after life and the wisdom it imparts to us.

Embarking on the journey to a chosen afterlife destination is a deeply personal and spiritual endeavor. It involves exploring your beliefs, values, and principles and aligning your life with those convictions. Whether you follow a traditional religious path, embrace a spiritual continuation concept, or craft a unique belief system, the journey to your chosen afterlife destination is a lifelong process of self-discovery, growth, and connection with the divine or spiritual. Ultimately, it's a voyage that reflects your deepest aspirations and the desire for a meaningful existence beyond this earthly life.

10.2 Embracing the Unknowable

The journey after life, as explored through the lenses of different belief systems and philosophies, reveals the profound humility of human existence. It reminds us that, despite our advances in science and technology, there remain aspects of life that are unknowable and beyond the reach of our empirical understanding.

This sense of mystery encourages us to approach life with a sense of wonder and curiosity, acknowledging that there are questions that may never be answered definitively. It invites us to respect diverse belief systems and philosophies, recognizing that the human quest for meaning takes many forms.

In the vast expanse of the universe, there exist realms of knowledge beyond the grasp of human understanding. From the mysteries of the cosmos to the depths of our consciousness, the universe unfolds its enigmas before us, inviting us to contemplate the profound concept of the unknowable. Embracing the unknowable is not an act of resignation but a courageous journey into the depths of uncertainty, challenging our perceptions and expanding the horizons of our wisdom. It is a celebration of the profound beauty found in life's mysteries and an acknowledgment of the limitations of our knowledge.

10.3 The Nature of the Unknowable

The unknowable encompasses a multitude of domains, from the nature of time and space to the origin of consciousness. It includes questions that have perplexed philosophers, scientists, and thinkers throughout history. What was there before the Big Bang? What is the true nature of reality? Can we ever fully understand the human mind? These inquiries remind us of the vastness of the unknown and the limitations of our current understanding.

10.4 The Humility of Not Knowing

Embracing the unknowable fosters humility. It acknowledges that the universe is far more complex and nuanced than our limited perceptions can comprehend. In this humility, there is a profound sense of awe and wonder. The realization that there are phenomena and truths beyond our current awareness humbles us, encouraging us to approach life with open-mindedness and receptivity.

10.5 Courage in Uncertainty

Navigating the unknown requires courage. It demands the bravery to confront our fears and uncertainties head-on, without the solace of definite answers. It is in this courage that we find resilience, adaptability, and the ability to thrive amidst life's uncertainties. Embracing the unknowable empowers us to accept change, to adapt to new circumstances, and to find strength in the face of the ever-shifting tides of life.

10.6 The Beauty of Mystery

The unknowable is not a void to be filled but a canvas upon which the art of curiosity and imagination can flourish. It is in the mystery of the cosmos that scientists find the drive to explore, discover, and innovate. It is in the enigma of the human psyche that artists, poets, and writers find inspiration for their creations. The beauty of mystery lies in its ability to evoke wonder, to spark the imagination, and to invite us to dream beyond the boundaries of what we know.

10.7 Embracing the Journey

Embracing the unknowable is not a destination but a journey—a continuous exploration of the mysteries that surround us. It is a mindset, a way of approaching life with a sense of wonder and curiosity. It encourages us to ask questions, to seek knowledge, and to marvel at the infinite complexities of the universe. In this embrace, there is freedom—the freedom to learn, to grow, and to appreciate the profound intricacies of existence.

In the grand tapestry of life, the threads of the unknowable are woven intricately, creating patterns of mystery and fascination. Embracing these mysteries with grace and courage enriches our human experience, reminding us that, in the face of the unknown, there is endless potential for discovery, understanding, and awe. As we journey forward, let us embrace the unknowable with open hearts and inquisitive minds, for it is in this embrace that the true essence of life's wonders is revealed.

10.8 The Importance of Ethical Living

In a world inundated with challenges and complexities, the significance of ethical living cannot be overstated. Ethical living encompasses a way of life that is guided by moral principles and conscientious choices, with the aim of creating a positive impact on both individuals and the broader society. It goes beyond personal conduct; it's a holistic approach that considers the welfare of all living beings, the environment, and future generations. Embracing ethical living nurtures compassion, empathy, and a profound sense of responsibility, thereby shaping a better world for everyone.

One common thread that runs through many interpretations of the journey after life is the emphasis on ethical living. Whether it's the concept of karma and its consequences in Eastern religions or the moral principles guiding monotheistic beliefs, the afterlife often serves as a moral compass, encouraging us to live with integrity, compassion, and kindness.

The idea that our actions in this life have repercussions in the next underscores the importance of responsible living. It calls us to consider the impact of our choices on ourselves, others, and the world at large. In this way, the journey after life serves as a reminder that our moral and ethical conduct has lasting significance.

10.9 Fostering Empathy and Compassion

Ethical living promotes empathy by encouraging individuals to consider the perspectives and experiences of others. By understanding the consequences of our actions on fellow humans, animals, and the environment, we cultivate a sense of compassion. This empathy forms the foundation for harmonious relationships, social cohesion, and a more compassionate society.

10.10 Preserving the Environment

Ethical living involves mindful consumption, sustainable practices, and environmental stewardship. With climate change and environmental degradation posing significant threats, ethical choices such as reducing waste, conserving energy, and supporting eco-friendly initiatives are crucial. By living ethically, we contribute to the preservation of our planet for future generations, ensuring they inherit a habitable and thriving environment.

10.11 Promoting Social Justice

Ethical living advocates for social justice and equality. It involves standing against discrimination, advocating for human rights, and supporting fair trade practices. By choosing ethically sourced products, supporting businesses that prioritize their employees' well-being, and engaging in activism, individuals can contribute to creating a more equitable world where everyone has access to opportunities and resources.

10.12 Enhancing Personal Well-being

Living ethically is not only beneficial to society and the environment but also to personal well-being. Engaging in ethical practices, such as volunteering, acts of kindness, and supporting charitable causes, brings a profound sense of fulfillment and purpose. Studies have shown that helping others and living in harmony with one's values enhance mental and emotional well-being, fostering a sense of inner peace and contentment.

10.13 Encouraging Responsible Consumption

Ethical living encourages responsible consumption habits. By being mindful of the products we buy, their origins, and their impact on the environment and society, we can contribute to reducing exploitation and unethical practices. Supporting companies and organizations that prioritize ethical production and social responsibility encourages a shift towards a more ethical marketplace.

10.14 Inspiring Positive Change

Living ethically sets an example for others. By demonstrating ethical values and making conscious choices, individuals inspire those around them to reflect on their own behaviors. Through collective efforts, societal norms can shift, leading to a widespread embrace of ethical living. This ripple effect can create a positive wave of change that transcends communities and borders.

In a world that often seems fragmented, ethical living serves as a unifying thread, connecting people through shared values and a collective commitment to a better future. It empowers individuals to recognize their interconnectedness with the world and to acknowledge the impact of their choices. By embracing ethical living, we not only enhance our own lives but also contribute to the creation of a more just, compassionate, and sustainable world for generations to come.

10.15 The Quest for Purpose and Fulfilment

For many, the journey after life is intimately tied to the search for purpose and fulfillment. Whether it's the pursuit of spiritual enlightenment, the quest for union with the divine, or the desire for personal growth and transformation, the afterlife provides a framework for understanding our place in the grand scheme of existence.

This quest for purpose challenges us to explore the depths of our own beliefs and values, encouraging us to align our actions with our deepest aspirations. It encourages us to seek meaning not only in the destination but also in the journey itself, recognizing that personal growth and self-discovery are essential aspects of the human experience.

10.16 Conclusion: An Ever-Evolving Exploration

The journey after life is an ever-evolving exploration, a reflection of humanity's enduring quest for meaning, understanding, and connection with the mysteries of existence. It transcends cultural, religious, and philosophical boundaries, uniting us in our shared curiosity about the great unknown.

As we conclude this reflection on the journey after life, let us embrace the uncertainty and wonder that it represents. ***Let us live ethically and authentically, guided by our deepest values and beliefs.*** And let us continue to explore the multifaceted tapestry of human spirituality and the eternal questions that define our existence, for the journey after life is a testament to the enduring curiosity and wisdom of the human spirit.

www.ingramcontent.com/pod-product-compliance
Lightning Source LLC
LaVergne TN
LVHW090123160826
845673LV00015B/824